THE NATURAL HISTORY of
Bumblebees

The Natural History of
Bumblebees
A Sourcebook for Investigations

Carol A. Kearns
and
James D. Thomson

University Press of Colorado

© 2001 by the University Press of Colorado

Published by the University Press of Colorado
5589 Arapahoe Avenue, Suite 206C
Boulder, Colorado 80303

The University Press of Colorado is a cooperative publishing enterprise supported, in part, by Adams State College, Colorado State University, Fort Lewis College, Mesa State College, Metropolitan State College of Denver, University of Colorado, University of Northern Colorado, University of Southern Colorado, and Western State College of Colorado.

The paper used in this publication meets the minimum requirements of the American National Standard for Information Sciences—Permanence of Paper for Printed Library Materials. ANSI Z39.48-1992

Library of Congress Cataloging-in-Publication Data

Kearns, Carol Ann, 1955–
    The natural history of bumblebees : a sourcebook for investigations / Carol A. Kearns and James D. Thomson.
        p. cm.
    Includes bibliographical references (p.   ).
    ISBN 0-87081-621-7 (pbk. : alk. paper) — ISBN 0-87081-565-2 (cloth : alk. paper)
    1. Bumblebees—Observers' manuals. I. Thomson, James D., 1950– II. Title.
    QL568.A6 K38 2001
    595.79'9—dc21

                            2001001001

10 09 08 07 06 05 04 03 02 01   10 9 8 7 6 5 4 3 2 1

to Jack and Joan Kearns

and

Barbara A. Thomson

Contents

Illustrations

Acknowledgments —————

We would especially like to acknowledge Barbara Thomson, who carefully edited and assisted with all stages of preparation. We also thank the American Museum of Natural History and the Museum of Comparative Zoology at Harvard University for the loan of bumblebee specimens. David Underwood at the University of Colorado helped us visualize the possibilities for the layout of the photographic field guide. This book would not have been possible without the insights and wisdom of many bumblebee biologists, past and present. Among our mentors and friends, we would particularly like to acknowledge Chris Plowright, Sarah Corbet, Robbin Thorp, Robin Owen, Karen Strickler, Michael Mesler, Izumi Washitani, and Masato Ono. The direct inspiration for developing the book came from a workshop for college teachers that we ran at the Rocky Mountain Biological Laboratory with David Inouye and Nick Waser. The enthusiasm and curiosity of the workshop participants stimulated us to begin the book in earnest.

Foreword

The Appeal of Bumblebees to Investigators of the Natural World

Everybody knows the burly, good-natured bumble-bee. Clothed in her lovely coat of fur, she is the life of the gay garden as well as of the modestly blooming wayside as she eagerly hums from flower to flower, diligently collecting nectar and pollen from the break to the close of day.

—F. W. Sladen, 1912

Can insects be *charming*? Sladen surely thought so, and even some people who dislike "bugs" in general make exceptions for bumblebees. As insects go, bumblebees are large and therefore easily observed. Their bright colors and intriguing behaviors have attracted the attention of naturalists over the last two centuries. They appear repeatedly in the classic pollination works of H. Müller (1883) and Knuth (1906–1909). Darwin had a particular fondness for bumblebees—which were called "humblebees" in his time—and spent a fair amount of time studying their habits. His work foreshadowed some current themes about keystone links within communities when he said, "The number of humblebees in any district depends in a great measure upon the number of fieldmice, which destroy their combs and nests . . . the number of mice is largely dependent, as everyone knows, on the number of cats . . . it is quite credible that the presence of a feline animal in large numbers in a district might determine, through the intervention first of mice and then of bees, the frequency of certain flowers in that district!" (Darwin 1859, p. 74).

Beyond his ecological speculations, Darwin (1859, 1878) was particularly interested in behavior. He described at length how bumblebees can pierce a flower's corolla tube to extract nectar without touching the reproductive floral parts. He also calculated the potential number of bee visits to flowers each day from his observations, and manipulated flowers to determine what features were of importance in attracting bumblebees. He became struck by the curious behavior of certain male bumblebees in his gardens at Down House, and although he never published this material, he kept notes from 1854 through 1861 (summarized by Freeman [1968]) about bees turning up at particular "buzzing places" that were used year after year. To track the movements of the bees as they commuted among these buzzing places, Darwin enlisted the aid of his substantial family. His notes conjure up an appealing picture of a flock of cheerful children in Victorian garb chasing bees about the hedgerows under the supervision of the greatest naturalist of all time: "The routes remain fixed within an inch. I was able to prove this by stationing five or six of my children each close to a buzzing place, and telling the one farthest away to shout out 'here is a bee' as soon as one was buzzing around. The others followed this up, so that the same cry of 'here is a bee' was passed on from child to child without interruption until the bees reached the buzzing place where I myself was standing."

Admittedly, Darwin spoils this nineteenth-century idyll a bit by mentioning the grimmer realities of field biology (and dropping in some jarringly casual terminology): "From the ivy leaf they went into a dry ditch which was covered over by a thick hedge and flew slowly along between the dense branches of thorn. I could only follow them along this ditch by making several of my children crawl in, and lie on their tummies. . . ."

We draw several lessons from this story. First, bumblebees do interesting things that can engage the curiosity of anyone from an eminent scientist to a schoolchild. Second, these behaviors can frequently be studied by simple observation without any elaborate equipment. Third, at least in Darwin's opinion, the value of such knowledge clearly outweighed the costs of soiling the waistcoats and pinafores of his offspring Willy, Etty, Georgy, Franky, Lenny, and (possibly) Bessy. Fourth, new things can still be discovered in this manner, and some of these will puzzle experts: despite correspondence with the "bee men" of his time, Darwin never resolved to his own satisfaction what these male bees were doing and how they recognized the buzzing places. In his field notes he did speculate that scent-marking was involved (". . . is it like dogs at cornerstones?"), but this conjecture was not confirmed until nearly a century later. Even today, basic aspects of bumblebee courtship and mating are poorly known for many species, but we are in the midst of a resurgence of scientific interest in these animals. In writing this book we hope to give both amateurs and beginning professionals enough basic knowledge to pursue more observations and investigations of these particularly amenable subjects. We particularly want to highlight the value of bumblebees for learning and teaching about animal behavior. As the use of vertebrate animals becomes more restricted, we feel that bumblebees can be a superior invertebrate model for investigating many basic components of behavior.

One may well ask whether this goal requires a new book; there is already a large, good literature available. Several major treatises on bumblebees were published in the 1900s, as well as a great deal of information relating to bumblebees that appeared in the scientific literature of entomology, foraging, animal behavior, and sociobiology. The scientific literature has been summarized in technical review articles by Morse (1982) and Plowright and Laverty (1984). English-language books devoted to bumblebee biology include Sladen's 1912 classic *The Humble-bee, Its Life History and How to Domesticate It;* Plath's 1934 *Bumblebees and Their Ways,* on North American species; Free and Butler's 1959 *Bumblebees* (British); Alford's 1975 *Bumblebees,* on the habits of British species; and Heinrich's 1979 *Bumblebee Economics,* which concentrates on energetics and foraging but also treats basic biology. Other major works that include keys, descriptions, or biogeographical data are Frison's 1927 "Records and Descriptions of Western [North American] Bumblebees," Franklin's 1912 "The Bombidae of the New World," Milliron's numerous works (1971–1973), taxonomic treatments by O. W. Richards (1968) and Ito (1985), and an annotated checklist of the world's *Bombus* species by P. H. Williams (1998). Recently, two British publications have been produced in response to the number of naturalists and schoolchildren interested in bumblebee natural history and conservation (Matheson 1996; Prys-Jones and Corbet 1991).

The classical books on natural history all cover much of the same material, but Sladen's is unique and indispensable. Fortunately, a new printing from Logaston Press is easily available through the International Bee Research Association (IBRA, see page 92). Although the book is old, the acuity of his observations remains unparalleled, and his delight in his subject shines through (as in the quotation at the beginning of our foreword). Sladen's descriptions of bees as "frightened," "pleased," "frantic," "furious," "drowsy," or "quarrelsome" are too anthropomorphic by modern standards, but few who observe them in their colonies will be able to refrain from using similar terms—if not perhaps in technical publications. A very attractive feature of the current edition is the inclusion of a facsimile of Sladen's first bumblebee book, an illustrated, handwritten manuscript that he "published" by stencil—at age sixteen—and sold for sixpence. This astonishing piece of childhood scholarship should inspire any youthful naturalist. By pairing Sladen's book with the excellent and up-to-date monograph by Prys-Jones and Corbet, a naturalist would have everything needed to begin serious studies on the British fauna. Both books include color plates and guides to identifying the species, although some of Sladen's names are out-of-date.

Unfortunately, North American students face additional barriers. Our bumblebee fauna is much larger, and although keys exist to aid with identification, they are regional and tend to use highly technical characters. The impetus for writing this book stemmed from a workshop on pollination biology for college teachers, sponsored by the United States National Science Foundation. We coordinated the workshop at the Rocky Mountain Biological Laboratory in Gothic, Colorado, in collaboration with Drs. David Inouye and Nick Waser. The workshop participants praised the book by Prys-Jones and Corbet, which we used as an introduction to bumblebee biology, and we all regretted the lack of a similar volume for North America. In addition, coauthor James Thomson, who has been working with bumblebees for more than twenty years, developed a series of activities based on Gothic's bumblebee species. These exercises were met with enthusiasm by workshop participants, some of whom adopted them for use in their own classes. We decided that a new niche existed for a book that would serve in part as a picture-based field guide for North American bumblebees and in part as a set of suggestions for studies and exercises. Our intent is to excite more general enthusiasm for these remarkable creatures. We know of a bumblebee survey conducted in Europe that employed schoolchildren with great success, providing useful information as well as helping children appreciate the role of bees and insects in the natural community (see Chapter 5). Similar North American projects involving the public are encouraged.

We are keenly aware of the limitations of our picture-matching approach for identifying species of bumblebees. Indeed, in most local areas a naturalist will encounter some very similar species that can be accurately distinguished only with difficulty and only by recourse to technical keys, dead specimens, and a good microscope. There is also quite a bit of geographical variability in the coat colors of some species. And finally, not all of the taxonomy of bumblebees is settled (P. H. Williams 1998). In the face of these difficulties, no set of pictures can suffice to identify every individual encountered. Nevertheless, we believe that most amateurs will be able to attach accurate names to at least several of the species they encounter. If we may draw an analogy to bird identification, some bumblebee species are distinctive and easily recognized even from a fleeting glance in the field; others, like *Empidonax* flycatchers, or Peterson's (1947) famous "Confusing Fall Warblers," will frequently be baffling to all except advanced students with special knowledge. We hope that this state of affairs will not deter interested naturalists from taking up the pursuit. If the birding analogy holds, we may even hope to infect some true enthusiasts who rise to the challenge of the difficult identifications.

On a more sober note, we must acknowledge that bumblebees can and do sting humans, that some of the North American species are not as "good-natured" as Sladen's British subjects, and that the consequences of being stung can be lethal if one is allergic. Therefore, please read the section on safety before starting out (Chapter 6).

The Natural History of
Bumblebees

1

INTRODUCTION

To make a prairie it takes a clover and one bee,
One clover, and a bee,
And revery.
The revery alone will do,
If bees are few.

—EMILY DICKINSON

Ernest Thompson Seton's classic *Wild Animals I Have Known* (1898, 1991) is a collection of stories that captured the attention of previous generations of children with realistic, if sentimental, accounts of the lives, struggles, and deaths of individual wild mammals and birds. In this spirit we begin with accounts of two bumblebee workers that presented us with striking responses to traumatic events in their lives.

Bombus affinis Yellow was an individually paint-marked member of a colony that was set out at a field site in Maine to examine the way in which bumblebees foraged and used space (Thomson, Peterson, and Harder 1987). For nearly two weeks, observers tracked her movements as she left the colony box, flew a regular foraging circuit or "trapline" within a stand of mapped plants, and returned home with pollen and nectar for the brood. Compared to others from the same colony, she was unusually systematic, deliberate, and easy to follow, and she became a favorite of the observers who spent hours in her company. Finally the end of the field season arrived. It was time to pack up the colony to return to New York, but Yellow did not return from her last afternoon trip. At the insistence of a particularly softhearted member of the team, we waited until well after dark, but Yellow did not appear. We reluctantly gave her up as lost, closed the colony, and packed it for travel. As we drove away the next morning, the same softhearted team member insisted that we make a detour to check the site one last time. We immediately found Yellow at the former nest location, doggedly flying back and forth in search of her home. We netted her and returned her to her sisters, and she "passed away quietly at home" back in New York.

Bombus flavifrons Blue-White was a free-foraging wild bee that had become accustomed to feeding from a set of potted plants of *Penstemon strictus* at Irwin, Colorado, a site 10,500 feet (3,200 m) high in the Rocky Mountains. For an exercise in the workshop mentioned in the Foreword, we put about twenty of these potted plants in the back of a pickup truck and transported them to Gothic, Colorado, a site that is about 1,000 feet lower (300 m), 8.5 miles away, and separated from Irwin by two ranges of 12,000-foot (4,000 m) mountains. As we unpacked the plants at Gothic, we noticed that Blue-White had stowed away in the truck. Sentimentality suggested that she too should be caught and repatriated, but this time a sterner scientific attitude prevailed, and we decided simply to see what would happen. In fact, Blue-White continued to forage at the potted *Penstemon* plants for days. She would accumulate visible loads of pollen on her legs; then she would disappear for a time; then she would reappear without her loads and begin foraging again. All of this is normal for a bee who is returning loads to her home colony, but it seems immensely improbable that Blue-White was returning to her old home near Irwin. Even if she successfully navigated her way home once, is it reasonable that she would then return to feed miles away, when the Irwin site had plenty of flowers? But if she were not returning to a hive somewhere, where was she dropping off her pollen loads? Possibly she had discovered, and been adopted by, a different colony near Gothic; such things happen. Possibly she simply dumped her loads when they became too heavy to carry. Until someone does a great deal of careful experimental work, we can only speculate about the relative likelihoods of these possibilities.

We hope that these two true tales will start our readers thinking about bumblebees as individuals who encounter problems. They react to these problems in various ways, but usually based on past experiences and always with tenacity. Having planted these seeds, we now turn to a brief summary of the natural history of this group of animals.

Bumblebees are large, fuzzy, attractive bees, easily recognized by their size and color. Beneath their fur or pile, their cuticle is black, but patches of black and contrastingly colored hairs give them a vivid appearance. Black and yellow are the most frequent colors, but some species display additional patches of white, orange, or rufous red. Because adjacent body segments frequently have different-colored hair, they tend to look striped. In temperate climates, they are found throughout the summer buzzing about meadows and gardens, visiting a wide variety of flowers for nectar and pollen. In most cases, they are effective pollinators of the plants they visit. A few species reach the warm tropics, but species and individuals are more common in the cooler parts of the world, especially in the Northern Hemisphere.

Bumblebees are social insects, usually forming colonies of twenty to several hundred individuals comprising two generations: a mother and her numerous offspring. One of the most appealing aspects of bumblebee study is watching the activity in the nest. All developmental stages can be present simultaneously, from eggs to larvae, pupae, and adults. Tasks are divided among the adults, so one can see the queen laying eggs, feeding larvae, and maintaining the hive, and foragers returning with loads of pollen and nectar. The bumblebee colony bustles with varied forms of activity, which tend to show characteristic daily rhythms.

Pollinators, including bumblebees, are of great interest to conservation biologists. As more habitat is converted to human use, patches of natural vegetation diminish. Pollinators, dependent on flowers for pollen and nectar, decrease in numbers as their food resources diminish, and their nesting habitat is lost. Many species of pollinators are in decline and several are threatened with extinction. Declines in bumblebees have been documented in several parts of the world.

Pollinators play critical ecological roles in communities. Without adequate pollination, many plants will produce fewer seeds and fruits. Seeds represent new generations of plants. Seeds, fruits, and plants provide nourishment and shelter for other members of natural communities, and provide food and resources for humans. Clearly, pollinators are critical to maintaining healthy ecosystems. The study of bumblebees yields information about pollinators and increases our awareness of the critical relationships between organisms within both natural communities and those altered by humans.

Bee Classification

Bees are insects and, like other insects, are creatures with exoskeletons and segmented bodies. The segments are fused into three basic body regions: the head, the thorax, and the abdomen. Adult insects generally have two antennae, two compound eyes and three ocelli (small, simple eyes) on the head, plus six legs and two pairs of wings on the thorax. (Some insects show variations on this basic body plan; e.g., flies have one pair of wings and a second set of highly reduced wing remnants; and some insects, like ants, have wingless forms.) Bees, ants, and wasps comprise the fourth-largest insect order, the Hymenoptera (Table 1-1).

On Being a Bee

Hymenoptera. Winged hymenopterans have two pairs of wings, a larger set in front and a smaller pair of hind wings. The front and hind wings are hinged together with a row of tiny hooks, a character distinguishing this group from the other winged insects.

Table 1-1—*Classification of Bumblebees*

KINGDOM:	Animalia
PHYLUM:	Arthropoda
CLASS:	Hexapoda (Insecta)
ORDER:	Hymenoptera—ants, bees, and wasps
SUPERFAMILY:	Apoidea—bees and sphecoid wasps
FAMILY:	Apidae
SUBFAMILY:	Apinae—honeybees, bumblebees, euglossine and meliponine bees
TRIBE:	Bombini—(Bombus and Psithyrus); Moderate- to large-sized bees. Distinguished from honeybees by size, presence of hind tibial spurs, and lack of hair on the eyes. Nonmetallic, with hairy thorax and abdomen. Black cuticle with colored pile.
GENUS:	*Bombus*

Note: Column headings are as follows:
(1) Nesting Preference: + (above ground), – (below ground), * (variable);
(2) Mode of Feeding Larvae: P (pocket-makers), NP (non-pocket-makers);
(3) Tongue Length: L (long), M (medium), S (short), NR (nectar robber); and
(4) Seasonality: E (tending to appear early), L (tending to appear late), Y (in flight all year).

Species	(1)	(2)	(3)	(4)	Range
GENUS *BOMBUS*					
SUBGENUS *ALPINOBOMBUS* SKORIKOV					
balteatus Dahlbom	–	P		L	Holarctic; Arctic AK and Canada, south on principal cordillera of west
balteatus (*kirbyellus* Curtis)			L		N. Am. to CA (Sierra Nevada Mts., White Mts.) and New Mexico (Truchas Peak); ? AZ (Patagonia Mts.)
hyperboreus Schönherr					Holarctic (circumpolar); Arctic AK and Canada (Yukon and N.W.T.); Greenland
neoboreus Sladen (*strenuus* Cresson)					AK, Yukon, N.W.T., south to B.C., ? Alta.
polaris Curtis			L		Holarctic (circumpolar); Arctic AK, Canada Greenland, parts of Arctic Eurasia
SUBGENUS *BOMBIAS* ROBERTSON					
auricomus (Robertson)					Ont. to FL, west to TX, OK, CO, WY, MT and southern Canada (Sask., Alta. B.C.)
nevadensis Cresson					AK south to CA, AZ, NM, and east to WS; Mexico
SUBGENUS *BOMBUS* LATREILLE S. STR.					
affinis Cresson		N	S, NR		Que. and Ont. south to GA, west to SD and ND
lucorum (Linnaeus)			NR		Holarctic; AK southward to parts of south B.C. and Alta., east through Yukon and N.W.T.

continued on next page

Table 1-1—*continued*

Species	(1)	(2)	(3)	(4)	Range
SUBGENUS *BOMBUS* LATREILLE S. STR. (*contd.*)					
terricola Kirby	*		S, NR	E	N.S. to FL, west to B.C., MT, and SD
(*terricola occidentalis* Greene)	–	N	S, NR	E	AK south to northern CA, NV, AZ, NM, SD
franklini (Frison)					Coastal OR
SUBGENUS *CROTCHIIBOMBUS* FRANKLIN					
crotchii Cresson				E	CA; Mexico (Baja California)
SUBGENUS *CULLUMANOBOM-BUS* VOGT					
rufocinctus Cresson	+	N		L	N.S., N.B., Que., west to B.C.., south to CA, AZ, NM, KS, MN, IL, MI, NY, VT, ME; Mexico (Distrito Federal, Hidalgo, Mex., Michoacan, Morelos, Sonora)
SUBGENUS *FERVIDOBOMBUS* SKORIKOV					
fervidus (Fabricius)	*	P	L	L	Que. and N.B. south to GA, west to B.C., WA, OR, CA; Mexico (Chihuahua)
fervidus (*californicus* Smith)	*	P		L	B.C. and Alta., south to CA, AZ, NM, Mexico (Baja California and Sonora)
pensylvanicus (Degeer)	+	P		E	Que. and Ont., south to FL, west to MN, SD, NE, CO, NM; Mexico and possible Centr. Am.
(*pensylvanicus sonorous* Say)				Y	TX, west to CA; Mexico
SUBGENUS *FRATERNOBOMBUS* SKORIKOV					
fraternus (Smith)				E	NJ to FL, west to ND, SD, NE, CO, NM
SUBGENUS *PYROBOMBUS* DALLA TORRE					
bifarius Cresson	–		S	E	B.C., OR, CA (Sierra Nevada Mts.), ID, UT, CO
(*bifarius nearcticus* Handlirsch)	–			E	AK, Yukon, south to CA (Sierra Nevada Mts.), UT
bimaculatus Cresson	+	N	L	E	Ont., ME, south to FL, west to IL, KS, OK, MS
caliginosus Frison					WA, OR, CA, generally coast, but also San Jacinto Mts.
centralis Cresson				E	B.C., Alta., south to CA, AZ, NM
flavifrons Cresson	–		M		AK, south to CA, ID, UT
(*flavifrons dimidiatus* Ashmead)					south B.C. to CA
flavifrons (*pleuralis* Nylander)					B.C., N.W.T., Yukon, AK, Rocky Mt. states

continued on next page

Table 1-1—*continued*

Species	(1)	(2)	(3)	(4)	Range
SUBGENUS *PYROBOMBUS* DALLA TORRE (*contd.*)					
frigidus Smith	*		S	E	AK, N.W.T., south at high elev. to CO
huntii Greene	–			E	B.C., Alta., south to CA, NV, UT, NM
impatiens Cresson	–	N	S	L	Ont., ME, south to FL, west to MI, IL, KS, MS
lapponicus (Fabricius) (*sylvicola* Kirby)	*		S		AK, east to Newf., south on the principal cordillera of western U.S. to CA, NV, UT, NM
melanopygus Nylander					OR, CA, NV (Douglas and Washoe Counties)
melanopygus (*edwardsii* Cresson)					
mixtus Cresson	+				AK, south to CA, ID, CO
perplexus Cresson	–	N	M		AK, ME, south to WI, IL, FL
sandersoni Franklin					Ont. to Newf., south to TN, NC
sitkensis Nylander					AK, south to CA, ID, MT, WY
ternarius Say	–	N	S	E	Yukon east to N.S., south to GA, MI, KS, MT, B.C.
vagans Smith	*	N	M	L	B.C. east to N.S., south to GA, TN, SD, MT, ID, WA
vandykei (Frison)					WA to southern CA
vosnesenskii Radoszkowski					B.C. south to CA, NV (Washoe County); Mexico (Baja California)
SUBGENUS *SEPARATOBOMBUS* FRISON					
griseocollis (Degeer)			S	E	Que. south to FL, west to B.C., WA, OR, northern CA
morrisoni Cresson				L	B.C. to CA, east to SD, NE, CO, NM
SUBGENUS *SUBTERRANEOBOMBUS* VOGT					
appositus Cresson	*	P	L	L	B.C. east to Sask., south to NM, AZ, CA (Cascades and Sierra Nevada Mts.)
borealis Kirby	*	P		L	southern Canada from N.S. to Alta. and northern U.S. from ME to NJ, west to ND and SD
GENUS *PSITHYRUS*					
ashtoni (Cresson)					P.E.I. west to Sask., south to ND, MN, WI, MI, OH, WV, VA
citrinus (Smith)					P.E.I. and N.B., south to FL, AL, west to SD, ND

continued on next page

Table 1-1—*continued*

Species	(1)	(2)	(3)	(4)	Range
GENUS *PSITHYRUS* (*contd.*)					
fernaldae (Franklin)					AK and Canada, south to NC, TN in east U.S., CO, CA in western U.S.
insularis (Smith)					Canada, south to CA, AZ (Oak Creek Canyon), NM, NE (Sioux County), NY (Ithaca), NH (Durham), ? AK (Berg Bay)
suckleyi Greene					AK, south to CA, UT, CO
variabilis (Cresson)					OH south to FL, west to ND, SD, NE, KS, OK, TX, NM, Mexico (Orizaba)

Abbreviations: Alta. (Alberta), B.C. (British Columbia), N.B. (New Brunswick), Newf. (Newfoundland), N.S. (Nova Scotia), N.W.T. (Northwest Territories), Ont. (Ontario), P.E.I. (Prince Edward Island), Que. (Quebec), and Sask. (Saskatchewan).

Authors' Notes: This table contains many blank cells. This indicates a need for more research and more compilation of unpublished information regarding the habits of different bumblebee species.

Our primary taxonomic reference is the paper by Paul Williams (1998). You will note that many species names are followed by a second name in parentheses. The names in parentheses are names you are likely to come across in the literature, and we have included them with the species currently recognized in the Williams 1998 paper. As Williams notes in this paper, there are a number of instances in which further taxonomic research "is urgently needed." R. Owen (personal communication) fervently agrees that a great deal remains to be worked out in this area. Just to illustrate one example, *B. fervidus* and the old species *B. californicus* are currently both lumped together under *B. fervidus. Fervidus,* however, has a haploid chromosome number of 18 and *californicus* has a haploid number of 19 (Owen et al. 1995). We hope some of our readers will rise to the challenge posed by Williams (1998).

Taxonomic References:
Williams 1998 (primary source); also Franklin 1912; Frison 1927; Hanson and Gauld 1995; Heinrich 1979; Krombein et al. 1979; Labougle 1990; Michener 2000; Michener et al. 1994; Milliron 1971–1973; Thorp, Horning, and Dunning 1983; Williams 1985

Pocket-Making References:
NOTE: Most species will store pollen when there is surplus.
Hobbes 1967, 1966 a and b, 1965 a and b, 1964; Milliron 1971, 1972, 1973; Plath 1927.

Nesting Preferences:
NOTE: There is considerable variation in nesting sites within species that may relate to the availability of suitable, cozy nest sites. Many species will happily nest in birdhouses, cracks in walls, or other artifacts when they are available. Modern fiberglass insulation is attractive to some species. This table indicates tendencies. In studies of most species, however, some percentage of nests do not fit the pattern.
Hobbs 1967, 1966 a and b, 1965 a and b, 1964; Milliron 1973, 1972, 1971; Plath 1927; Richards 1978.

Seasonality:
Plath 1934; Hobbes 1964–1967; Milliron 1973, 1972, 1971

Range Information:
Krombein et al. 1979 (primary source); also Franklin 1912; Milliron 1971, 1973 a and b; Williams 1998.

The mode of sex determination is an unusual feature of the Hymenoptera. The egg-laying queen can fertilize her eggs with sperm stored at the time of mating in a special organ called the spermatheca. If she does this, the eggs will develop into diploid (having two copies of each gene) individuals carrying genes from the queen and her mate. Unfertilized eggs will develop as well, however, and become haploid individuals (having only one copy of each gene) carrying only genes derived from the queen. Unfertilized eggs always develop into males. Females are produced as a result of heterozygosity at one or more of the sex-determination genes (there may be several in bees). The majority of fertilized eggs will have at least one heterozygous sex gene, and so most fertilized eggs produce females. A small percentage of diploid individuals are likely to be homozygous at all the sex-determining loci, and these individuals will be males even though they are diploid. (For a more detailed discussion of diploid male production, see Owen and Packer 1994.)

Bees have two pairs of wings and branched body hairs. The presence of wings in sterile workers distinguishes bees from ants. Ants of the sterile, working castes are wingless, although reproductive males and females are winged. The presence of branched hairs distinguishes bees from other hymenopterans whose hairs are single, unbranched strands. The majority of bees exist on a purely floral diet of pollen and nectar throughout their lives, from larvae to adults. There are seven families of bees (Michener 2000), grouped by morphological variations of the wings, tongue, and pollen-carrying apparatus.

Superfamily Apoidea. The Apoidea is the superfamily that includes bees and sphecoid wasps. Morphological characteristics of the thorax, developmental features, and nesting habits unite the insects within this group. Bees and sphecoid wasps, however, differ in a number of behavioral and morphological features. With some exceptions, wasps are predators. Females use their stings to paralyze prey, then provision their nests with their victims. Adult wasps feed on fluids that exude from their prey, and supplement their diet with sugars obtained from the nectar of flowers. In contrast, bees feed on honey and pollen throughout their life cycle. Having a floral diet eliminates the need to paralyze prey, so bees reserve the use of their stingers for defense. Besides the branched hairs already mentioned, which set bees apart from other hymenopterans, one can distinguish sphecoid wasps from bees most quickly by examining their facial hair. Sphecoid wasps have shiny faces because of the presence of golden or silvery hairs. If bees have hair on their faces, it is branched and does not appear shiny. Females of most bee species have specialized structures on the legs for pollen-carrying; wasps lack these morphological features. There are exceptions to the rule, however: parasitic bees, robber bees, highly eusocial queens, and bees (such as *Hylaeus*) that carry pollen solely in their crops lack the specialized leg structures. Bees are probably descendants of the hunting wasps in the family Sphecidae. Sugar-loving bees apparently evolved from sphecoids similar to modern *Psenulus* wasps, a group that preys on aphids and incorporates aphid honeydew into the adult diet (O'Toole and Raw 1991). The seven families of bees within the Apoidea comprise an estimated twenty thousand different species, and following more detailed molecular and morphological work that separates cryptic species, that number is likely to rise (Michener 2000).

Family Apidae, Subfamily Apinae: Bumblebees belong to the subfamily Apinae of the family Apidae (Michener 2000). Within this subfamily are several tribes of corbiculate bees, including the honeybees, bumblebees, stingless tropical honeybees, and tropical euglossine bees. Corbiculate bees have smooth, concave areas on the outer side of the hind leg, also known as pollen baskets; they carry their pollen loads in these corbiculae. Long hairs that fringe the corbicula hold the pollen in place. Most other types of bees carry pollen in less specialized areas of fur called scopae (Figure 1-1).

The subfamily Apinae contains the most social of the bees. Eusocial insects, like the bumblebee and honeybee, live in colonies that contain a reproductive queen and a caste of sterile female workers. Other divisions of labor exist among the worker bees, whose roles may include foraging, nest maintenance, and guard duty. Unlike the situation with ants, however, the division of labor among worker bees is behavioral only; there are no fixed morphological differences. Furthermore, workers may change their specializations as they age or as the colony's needs change.

Tribe Bombini: The Bombini comprises the bumblebees (*Bombus*) and cuckoo or parasitic bumblebees (*Psithyrus*). We have retained the term *Psithyrus* because of its usefulness in distinguishing parasitic bumblebees; Michener (2000) and P. H. Williams (1998) now recognize these parasitic forms as belonging to the genus *Bombus*, subgenus *Psithyrus*. This tribe, which is most diverse in temperate areas, consists of eusocial bees that construct wax nests.

Genus Bombus. The bumblebees are moderate- to large-sized, hairy, eusocial bees. Most bumblebees have black and yellow pile, often with additional areas of white, red, or orange. Females have broad, concave corbiculae surrounded by long, stiff hairs. The word *Bombus* means "booming" or "buzzing" in Latin.

Subgenera. The genus *Bombus* has been variously subdivided by different authors. In a highly disputed classification scheme, Milliron (1971–1973) divided the group into three separate genera with subgenera. Others have

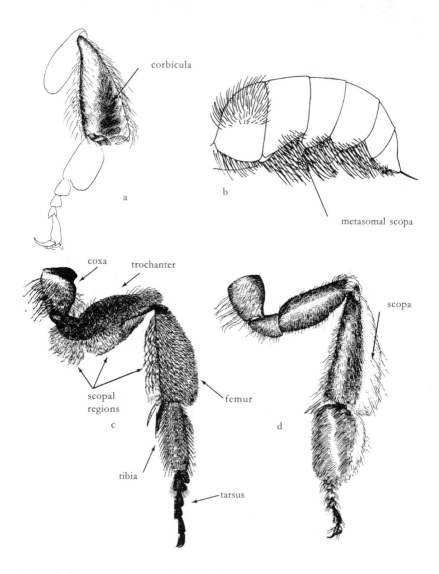

Fig. 1-1: Pollen carrying structures of female bees: (a) The corbicula of bumblebees and honeybees consists of a flat or concave surface on the hind tibia; the surface is generally flat and free of hairs. Stiff hairs surround the pollen-carrying surface. (b) The lower abdomen of most female Megachilidae bears specialized pollen-carrying hairs. (c) Many female bees have pollen-carrying hairs on the hind femur, and as in this illustration, they may have hairs on the trochanter and tibia as well. They carry pollen largely on the underside of the leg. Some of the Colletidae, Andrenidae, and Halictidae carry pollen this way. (d) Some bees have extensive pollen-carrying hairs on the hind tibia and few (or no) hairs on the femur and trochanter. Some of the Anthophoridae, Halictidae, and Andrenidae have this type of pollen-carrying structure. (Reprinted from Michener, McGinley, and Danforth, 1994, with permission.)

kept the single genus *Bombus*, but have named subgenera (O. W. Richards 1968; Ito 1985). Ito's paper reviews the earlier classification schemes and provides a framework for understanding the controversies. The thirteen recognized subgenera of North and Central America are "weakly differentiated groups" (Michener, McGinley, and Danforth 1994, 168), but are sometimes useful in categorizing nesting preferences and in determining ease of colony maintenance in captivity, as there appear to be behavioral similarities within groups. It seems likely that the subgeneric classification will require some changes as good molecular-genetic data clarify species relationships. The most recent checklist of bumblebee species was prepared by Paul H. Williams in 1998 (P. H. Williams 1998). Our classification follows Williams's scheme with the exception that we retain the widely used generic name *Psithyrus* for the social parasites (Table 1-1).

Genus Psithyrus. *Psithyrus* are "cuckoo" bumblebees that develop as social parasites in *Bombus* nests. Fertilized *Psithyrus* females take over thriving bumblebee colonies by killing or subduing the resident queen. The *Psithyrus* queen begins laying her own eggs within the colony. The *Bombus* workers feed her and nurture her developing brood. *Psithyrus* larvae emerge as male or female reproductive forms, never as worker bees.

Psithyrus bees are large, black and yellow, or (rarely) all black. They are generally less hairy than *Bombus*, often showing patches of exposed black cuticle on their abdomen. *Psithyrus* queens lack corbiculae; these structures are unnecessary because these bees never collect pollen for their broods. They have thick cuticular armor and robust stingers, both of which presumably help them in combat with *Bombus* queens. Their abdomens are incurved, which may give them an advantage over *Bombus* in stinging fights. The word *Psithyrus* means "murmuring" in Latin, and refers to the relatively soft buzzing sound produced by these bees.

Patterns of Social Behavior Among Bees

Bumblebees dwell in colonies, and their social interactions and varied roles and activities within the colony are features that make bumblebee study so interesting. Among all species of bees, however, this pattern of cooperation, interaction, and division of labor is rare, restricted largely to the Apidae (plus some Halictidae). The majority of bee species are solitary (O'Toole and Raw 1991).

Solitary bees typically emerge in late spring or early summer in temperate areas, or at the end of the rainy season in tropical regions. Males usually emerge first and begin searching for emerging females. After mating, females choose a nest site and start nest construction. Many solitary bee species are miners, excavating their nesting burrows in loose soil or sand

and lining the nest with glandular secretions. Others prefer preformed cavities such as hollow plant stems or holes formed by wood-boring beetles. Still others build nests on the surfaces of rocks and buildings. Bees in the latter two categories generally line their nests with mud, leaves, resins, or other materials they have collected.

A female solitary bee forms a cell in which to lay her first egg. She then provisions the cell with a mass of pollen and nectar that will sustain the offspring until it is ready to pupate. It may take many foraging trips to accumulate a large enough supply. When the provision is ready, she lays an egg and then seals off the cell. During this process, cells are vulnerable to invasion by various "cleptoparasitic" bees and wasps, who lay their own eggs on the provision mass. After finishing her first cell, the nesting bee goes on to produce as many as eight to fourteen cells (Wilson 1971). Although she may contain more than twice that many fertilized eggs, she does not lay them all. The female usually dies before her offspring emerge, so there is no overlap of generations or interaction between larvae and adults.

Although the majority of bees are solitary, some species show different degrees of social interaction between adults, or between adults and offspring. We describe several different levels of sociality below. Bear in mind that even within one bee species, there can be variation in the degree of social behavior at different stages of colony development and among different populations (Michener 2000; O'Toole and Raw 1991; Wilson 1971).

The simplest level of association is an aggregation that results when solitary females build nests close together in the same area (O'Toole and Raw 1991). This could result from females returning to their natal site to nest, or from some innate attraction to bees of the same species. If good nesting sites are limited, females may be compelled to nest in close proximity. In several instances where aggregations occur, however, researchers have located what appear to be suitable nesting sites in abundance close to the aggregation. Aggregated nesting is common.

Parasociality involves interactions among females of the same generation. Parasociality comprises three categories: communality, quasisociality, and semisociality (Michener 2000). Casual observations of a small colony will not be enough to demonstrate the form of interaction among the adult female bees, making this inclusive term an appropriate choice. Communal nesting occurs when several females share a common nest entrance that leads into separate nests for each female. There is no cooperation among females and no tolerance for other females that venture too close to an individual's nest. The females are all of the same generation and are probably sisters. The advantage of communal nesting is most likely the continual presence of a bee guarding the nest entrance. Truly solitary bees must leave their nests unguarded when they forage. Communal nesting is common in the families Andrenidae and Megachilidae, and subfamilies Halictinae and Nomiinae in the Halictidae (O'Toole and Raw 1991).

Quasisociality is a less commonly used term (Michener 2000) that refers to bees of the same generation that not only tolerate each other but also cooperate in nest construction. This condition may represent a stage in colony development or an occasional situation found in some populations of a species, rather than a discrete form of social behavior (Michener 2000, 1974). In quasisocial colonies, all of the cooperating females are mated and have developed ovaries. They construct, line, and provision a single nest, but only one female lays an egg in each cell. A quasisocial nest looks much like a communal nest, and so we have very few documented examples of quasisocial bees. This form of behavior seems to exist, at least at times, among some euglossine bees (*Euglossa* and *Eulaema*) as well as some species of *Nomia* (Halictidae) and *Osmia* (Megachilidae) (Michener 1974).

Semisocial bees also work cooperatively to form a single nest in which multiple females lay eggs. Some of the females have undeveloped ovaries, though, and these bees specialize as foragers. Those females capable of laying eggs spend little time foraging, so there is some division of roles among the females of one generation. This degree of sociality seems to occur occasionally among some species that are generally communal or quasisocial. Semisociality may be the norm in *Augochloropsis sparsilis* and among some *Pseudaugochloropsis* species (Halictidae; O'Toole and Raw 1991).

The term subsocial behavior emphasizes the presence of interactions between generations of bees, rather than between cooperating females of the same generation. Unlike the parasocial bees, subsocial female bees guard their eggs, tend their larvae, and clean their nests. Instead of mass provisioning cells, the females of some species feed their larvae repeatedly throughout their development. Subsocial bees include some of the dwarf carpenter bees (*Ceratina, Allodape, Exoneurella*; Apidae, subfamily Xylocopinae; O'Toole and Raw 1991).

The fundamental features of eusociality are overlapping adult generations, cooperative brood care, and presence of sterile workers. Queens lay eggs and become dependent on workers to supply food. Workers forsake their own reproduction and perform tasks essential to the development of a strong colony that can produce reproductive bees. Eusociality has long provoked serious concern among evolutionary biologists: the existence of sterile castes, at first glance, runs counter to the theory of evolution by natural selection (O'Toole and Raw 1991). In *The Origin of Species*, Darwin refers to eusociality as "one special difficulty, which at first appeared to me insuperable, and actually fatal to the whole theory of evolution by natural selection." Yet, he concludes that "this difficulty, though appearing insuperable, is lessened, or, as I believe, disappears, when it is remembered that selection may be applied to the family, as well as to the individual, and may thus gain the desired end" (Darwin 1859, 236–237). With this statement he foreshadows the extensive literature since the 1960s relating to kin selection and the evolution of cooperative behavior.

The paradox of sterility among workers is most often explained by reference to kin selection. The theory of kin selection seeks to explain cooperation and conflict among related organisms that share many genes (Hamilton 1972). The principal insight of the theory is that one must think about the success of genes, not simply the success of individuals. Suppose that a new gene arises in a population. Will that gene spread and increase in frequency, or will it be weeded out by natural selection? Ordinarily we would expect a gene that abolishes any particular individual's reproductive output to be eliminated; the affected individual obviously cannot pass the gene on to the next generation. If, however, the same gene also increases the reproductive success of that individual's relatives ("kin"), the gene may spread after all. By definition, close relatives share genes. If a nonreproducing female helps a sister to succeed and reproduce, her genes may be passed on successfully if her nieces and nephews are sufficiently numerous. In haplodiploid systems, full sisters share 75 percent of their genes with each other and only 50 percent of their genes with their mother. This is because females have a full, identical set of genes from their haploid fathers, and share an average of 50 percent of the genes inherited from their mothers. Thus sister bees, ants, or wasps are more closely related to each other than they are to their mothers. Although she may be sterile, a worker bee can substantially promote the continuance of her own genes by helping her reproductive sisters.

Note, however, that sociality has also arisen in some animals that lack haplodiploidy, such as termites and naked mole rats. Although the mechanism of kin selection clearly eases the evolution of sociality, it is not strictly necessary. Kin selection and benefits derived from cooperative nest defense and food collection may all be factors related to the development of highly social forms. It has also been shown that females frequently have multiple mates, so that their offspring may be half sibs; then the levels of relatedness in a colony are lower than the theory posits. The degree of sociality in different types of bees, wasps, and ants and the evolution of eusociality from solitary and quasisocial bees are topics of continued interest among biologists.

Primitively eusocial bees include bumblebees and sweat bees of the family Halictidae (O'Toole and Raw 1991). Colonies are generally formed by a single queen, and thus the colony proceeds from a solitary stage, to a subsocial stage, and on to a eusocial stage as it develops. Among some species, several queens may initiate the nest, but eventually one asserts herself and becomes the dominant egg-laying female. Morphological differences, especially in size, may exist between the queen and worker bees, but the queen must spend some portion of her life foraging and performing other "worker" tasks when the colony is young. Therefore she retains worker features. She is not as distinctly different from the workers as is the queen in highly eusocial species like honeybees.

Bumblebee colonies do not show the same level of organization, communication, and pheromonal control as seen in the highly eusocial bees. Adults do not directly feed each other, although they feed from common food stores. Among bumblebees it is not uncommon for workers to lay eggs. These eggs, should they survive, always develop into males because the workers are unfertilized. There can be conflict between the queen and workers: queens may eat worker eggs, and workers may eat queen eggs or reject larvae selectively, manipulating the sex ratio of offspring. Levels of reproductive suppression of workers by the queen seem to vary among species. In laboratory colonies of the Amazonian species *Bombus atratus*, worker bees produce most of the male eggs (Wilson 1971).

Highly eusocial bees include the honeybees (Tribe Apini) and the tropical stingless bees (Tribe Meliponini) in the subfamily Apinae of the Apidae. The queen is very distinct from her hundreds to thousands of sterile worker offspring. She is basically an egg-laying machine, completely dependent upon workers for even her own food. Her mouthparts, eyes, and antennae are all reduced, and she lacks structures associated with pollen collection. The queen produces a strong pheromone that inhibits workers' ovaries from developing. Honeybees are in constant communication with other members of the colony via visual, tactile, and pheromonal communication. Workers regularly feed and groom each other, and pheromones are passed among all individuals of the colony. Among highly eusocial bees, new colonies are formed by a queen accompanied by a swarm of workers.

On Being a Bumblebee

Bumblebee Morphology. Bumblebees are among the largest bees common in the temperate zone. They are generally about 15–25 mm long, but size is variable even within a species and caste. Workers produced early in the season may be smaller than honeybees, but late-summer workers tend to be larger, and new queens are quite large. The queen of the largest known bumblebee, *Bombus dahlbomii* of South America, is over 30 mm long. In North America, the only other bee genera with such large individuals are

Xylocopa (carpenter bees) and some *Anthophora*. Bumblebees are readily distinguished from carpenter bees by their hairy abdomens. Carpenter bees have blue-black abdomens with few hairs. Bees of the genus *Anthophora* have a hairless, dorsal triangular plate on the last abdominal segment. They are hairy bees, generally brownish in color, that do not live in colonies. (Both *Anthophora* and *Xylocopa* are interesting bees, and perhaps less well studied than bumblebees, so the reader is encouraged to investigate their activities, too. Most of the suggested research projects in Chapter 7 could be applied to these bees as well as to bumblebees, although the nests are not as easy to observe. For studying *Xylocopa* nests in solid wood, researchers have actually used X-ray machines!)

If you examine a bumblebee closely under a dissecting microscope or with a hand lens, you will see the three main body parts characteristic of insects: head, thorax, and abdomen (Figure 1-2). The head bears two antennae, used for touch and "smell." Each has a basal scape and pedicel, followed by a flagellum made of ten segments in the female or eleven in the male. Thus the female has a total of twelve antennal segments and the male a total of thirteen (Figure 1-3). The front of the face, or clypeus, may be either long or short (Figure 1-3) depending on the species (Table 1-1). Face length is an important character for identifying bees by technical keys; it also gives ecological information. A long face is correlated with a long tongue, which can be used to lap nectar from deep corolla tubes. The tongue folds behind the head when the bee is not feeding and extends for lapping and

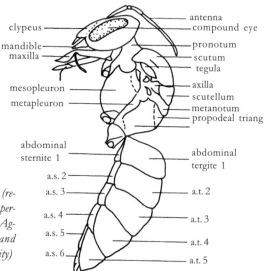

clypeus — antenna
— compound eye
mandible — pronotum
maxilla — scutum
— tegula
mesopleuron — axilla
metapleuron — scutellum
— metanotum
— propodeal triang

abdominal
sternite 1 — abdominal
tergite 1
a.s. 2

Fig. 1-2: Bee gross morphology (redrawn from Mitchell 1960 with permission from North Carolina Agricultural Research Service and North Carolina State University)

a.s. 3 — a.t. 2
a.s. 4 — a.t. 3
a.s. 5
a.s. 6 — a.t. 4
— a.t. 5

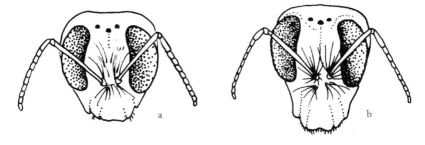

Fig. 1-3: Bee face and antennae: (a) A short-faced bee's face is roughly as long as it is wide. (b) A long-faced bee's face is longer than it is wide.

licking. The mandibles, or jaws, function in biting, working wax, and carrying larvae.

The thorax bears two pairs of membranous wings and six legs. The pair of wings on each side can be joined together by a row of tiny hooks (hamulae) on the hind wing. The hamulae catch in a fold at the rear of the forewing (Figure 1-4). Thus the wings can be free at rest, but hooked into a functional unit during flight. Although the legs, which have sharp terminal claws, naturally function in walking and in clinging to flowers, they are also adapted for raking up pollen from the bee's body or for scraping it directly out of flowers. The front legs each have a hollow groove, the antenna cleaner, at one of the joints (Figure 1-5). The bee can groom an antenna by pulling it through this groove, which is lined with fine hairs. Both hind legs of female *Bombus* bear large, concave, shiny areas surrounded by long, stiff hairs. These are the corbiculae, used for carrying pollen loads. Cuckoo bees of the genus *Psithyrus* and male bumblebees lack corbiculae. Female *Bombus* use their front legs to comb pollen from the body hairs where it collects when they visit flowers. The pollen is slightly moistened with nectar and formed into a paste. The front and middle legs push the paste into the corbiculae.

The abdomen comprises six segments in the female and seven in the male. Internally the abdomen contains a fat body, a structure most pronounced in queens, less so in workers, and nearly lacking in males. The fat body serves as a food reserve and is most important for young queens that must hibernate over winter. When the young queen first enters hibernation, the fat body may fill most of the abdomen. Little of it will remain when she emerges in the spring. Females also contain wax glands within the abdomen, and they can extrude wax from between segments of the ventral surface. The wax is used in construction of brood cells, storage vessels, and other components of nest architecture. The composition of the wax differs from

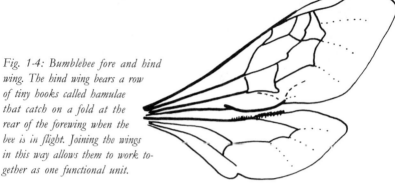

Fig. 1-4: Bumblebee fore and hind wing. The hind wing bears a row of tiny hooks called hamulae that catch on a fold at the rear of the forewing when the bee is in flight. Joining the wings in this way allows them to work together as one functional unit.

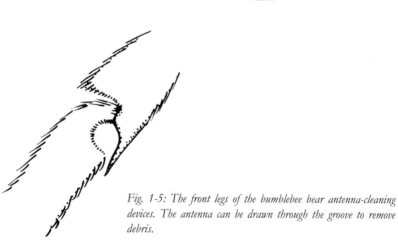

Fig. 1-5: The front legs of the bumblebee bear antenna-cleaning devices. The antenna can be drawn through the groove to remove debris.

that of honeybee wax, with a significantly lower melting point of about 35–45°C. The tip of the abdomen bears a stinger, a modified ovipositor used for colony defense. Unlike the stinger of the honeybee, its tip is not barbed; bumblebees do not lose the stinger after use, but can sting repeatedly. Fortunately they are generally less aggressive than honeybees, and multiple stings from a single bee are unlikely.

Queens are generally noticeably larger than worker bees, although there may be overlap in size range. With a few exceptions, such as *Bombus affinis* and the Central American *B. ephippiatus,* the color patterns of queens and workers are the same. Yet in some species, workers are variable in pattern (*B. crotchii, B. flavifrons, B. rufocinctus, B. sandersoni;* Heinrich 1979). Males appear to have long antennae because of their extra segment. Other differences are variation in the number of abdominal segments visible from the dorsal view (seven in male, six in female); the lack of corbiculae on their slender, hairier legs; and the presence of male genitalia rather than a stinger (Photographs 1-1 to 1-3, pages 107–108; also see photographic key). The absence of a stinger obviously prohibits males from stinging people. If you are confident in your ability to sex bumblebees, you can really impress your friends by grabbing male bees from flowers using only your bare hands. Males are not produced until late summer and will not be seen early in the season. Within a species, males tend to have longer fur than females, and also tend to be more yellow. In the eastern United States and Canada, a yellow-faced bumblebee is probably a male.

Bumblebee Distribution

P. H. Williams (1998) recognized 239 valid species of bumblebees world-wide. Bumblebee distribution centers on the northern temperate zone, through Europe, Asia including Japan, and North America. In the United States there are about 50 species of *Bombus* or *Psithyrus*, although in any particular community there may be only four or five.

In general, bee diversity is greatest in warm, arid climates such as the Mediterranean and the deserts of the North American Southwest, but bumblebees tolerate colder temperatures and more adverse weather than most other bees. This is in part because of their size and shape. They have a large ratio of volume to surface area and thus do not cool down as rapidly as smaller bees. Bumblebees are also capable of muscular thermogenesis, which allows them to produce their own heat so they may continue flying and foraging at lower ambient temperatures than many insects. Their insulating pile also conserves metabolic heat. Bumblebees of high elevations and latitudes generally have longer, shaggier hair than low-elevation forms. These characteristics, combined with bumblebees' efficiency at pollen transport, make them important pollinators of high latitudes and high elevations, where few other insects can be as active. Several species are found near the Arctic Circle; others persist at the opposite extreme in Tierra del Fuego. They are generally common in high mountains of the world, even throughout the Tropics.

Some bumblebees do tolerate warmer conditions. A few species are found in the East Indian archipelago, and even in South America, including one common in tropical forests of the Amazon. Bumblebees are absent south of the Sahara in Africa, in India except in the northern highlands, and in the Caribbean. They have been introduced and become naturalized in New Zealand, Israel, Tasmania, possibly the Australian mainland, and Hawaii.

2

Annual Life Cycle

Bees in the late summer sun
Drone their song
Of yellow moons
Trimming black velvet,
Droning, droning a sleepysong.

—Carl Sandburg

The Queen–Colony Initiation

In northern temperate areas, bumblebee colonies follow an annual cycle. On a mild spring day, about the time when the first willow flowers appear, bumblebee queens emerge from their subterranean hibernation. The large queens are the only bees remaining from last summer's brood.

The newly emerged queen commences foraging. She needs nectar for energy and pollen for completion of her own reproductive development and so she can prepare a food mass for her offspring. Willows are an important food for many bumblebee species, providing large quantities of pollen from the male catkins and nectar from flowers of both sexes. Many other spring flowers are used as well. Bumblebees are generalist feeders, in contrast to some solitary bees that collect pollen only from one or a few related species of plants.

At night, the queen rests in vegetation near her food plants. Her small ovaries and wax glands begin to develop and she becomes "broody," or ready to nest. The bumblebee queen must be able to perform all the tasks of a worker bee because she is the sole founder of the colony. Unlike honeybee queens, which have reduced mouthparts and eyes, short antennae, and no pollen-collecting hairs, bumblebee queens are completely functional. Morphologically, queens and workers differ only in size. Whereas bumblebee queens must be able to perform many tasks, honeybee queens have more limited behaviors. During a small portion of their life span they mate and challenge rival queens, after which time they function solely as egg producers.

The bumblebee queen must locate a suitable nesting site. Different bumblebee species prefer different sorts of nests; some deep below the ground, others directly on the surface (Table 1-1). Because the queens do not dig their own nests they seek a suitable crevice or hole. Many form their nests in old rodent burrows, or among the tall grasses in old mouse nests. Insulation and bedding are important. While searching for nests, queens are seen flying low to the ground, entering small openings among rocks, under logs, and even within stone walls, overturned flower pots, discarded mattresses, and other artificial objects. A queen may explore many surfaces before choosing a site, as the success of her brood depends on a good nest location. Finally she settles on a sunny, dry location. In the Northern Hemisphere, south-facing slopes are preferred. She hollows out a cavity about the size of a tennis ball and may add nectar to the inner nest material as a binding. If underground, she will also construct an entrance tunnel.

When the queen first leaves her new nest, she flies about the nest-site entrance in ever-widening circles before leaving the location. This orientation flight presumably helps her to remember landmarks so she can relocate the nest. Orientation flights continue for some time, then gradually diminish as the queen becomes more certain of the terrain.

The queen forages at flowers for nectar and pollen. When she is producing sufficient amounts of wax, she begins construction. Like all the worker bees, the queen has mandibles (jaws) designed for biting and manipulating materials such as wax. Her saliva can soften the wax so that it is easily manipulated. In the center of the nest she produces a wax cell in which she will lay her eggs. This may rest on top of a ball of pollen, or she may place pollen directly in the cell to provision her young. At about the same time, or sometimes after egg-laying, she also sculpts wax into a honeypot where she will store nectar. Initially the nectar pot serves as a reserve supply for the queen, who may consume it during the night or during periods of bad weather when she cannot forage. Later, additional honey pots will serve the entire colony (Photographs 2-1 to 2-4, pages 108–109).

Now the queen is ready to lay eggs. She was fertilized in the fall before her hibernation, and she stored the sperm in a storage organ called the spermatheca. Queen bees determine the sex of their offspring by whether or not they release stored sperm from the spermatheca to fertilize an egg as it is laid. As mentioned in Chapter 1, a fertilized egg develops into a diploid individual, usually female (see "Hymenoptera"), bearing two sets of chromosomes per cell, one set each from the mother and the father. An unfertilized egg develops into a haploid male with a single set of chromosomes per cell; his genetic makeup is derived solely from the queen. Early in colony development, the queen bumblebee fertilizes all her eggs to produce a pool of female worker bees.

The ancestral ovipositor of bees has been modified into a stinger and no longer functions in its original role. Instead the queen bee inserts her abdomen into the prepared egg cell with her stinger penetrating the pollen mass. Eggs are released from an opening at the tip of the abdomen. The queen deposits eight to fourteen pale, sausage-shaped eggs, 2.5 to 4 mm long. If the cell is not yet capped and she is laying her eggs on the pollen mound, she will proceed to cover the eggs with a wax roof. The queen incubates the eggs by lying on top of the wax and pollen structure. Her activity makes a depression in the top of the mound, called the incubation groove. Generally she faces toward the nest entrance with her honeypot in easy reach. She contracts her large flight muscles to generate heat, which is transferred from her thorax to her abdomen and finally to the egg clump. The sparsely haired undersurface of her abdomen is analogous to the brood patch of a bird. Ideal nest temperature is between 30 and 32°C. If the eggs are allowed to cool, development proceeds more slowly.

The eggs hatch in three to four days. Hatching of this "first brood" is highly synchronous. The larvae are then in a common cavity within the pollen and wax. The bumblebee larva has a head, three thoracic, and ten abdominal segments. It lacks legs, eyes, and hair; it has only fleshy lobes surrounding its mouth. Initially pale, it changes to pinkish gray or brown and passes through four larval stages or "instars" before pupation. During this time the larvae consume pollen provided by the queen. As they grow, each becomes walled off in a separate brood cell that grows along with the larva. The final size of the adult worker is related to the amount of food it consumes as a larva. The first brood tends to be small in terms of both the number and the size of individuals because only the queen is provisioning the larvae. (Presumably there is some advantage to producing workers quickly, because a lone queen and her nest are quite vulnerable. There may well be a trade-off involved between producing workers rapidly and foraging longer in order to produce large workers.) A colony that is starved later in development may also produce tiny workers. Captive colonies that are overfed may produce giant, queen-sized workers.

The queen uses one of two methods to feed the larvae. These methods are consistent within species, so some species are referred to as "pollen storers" and others as "pocket makers" (see Table 1-1; the pattern occasionally breaks down in captive colonies). The pollen storers keep a reserve supply of pollen available in the nest to feed the larvae. At later stages of colony development, this pollen is stored in old cocoons that have been modified by adding wax to increase their height. The queen (and later the workers) feed the larvae by biting a hole in the larval cell and regurgitating a mixture of pollen and honey into the cell. As the larvae grow, they form separate chambers and are fed individually.

Pocket makers build wax pockets adjacent to the larval cell and supply them with pollen, from which larvae feed directly. Pocket makers occasionally feed the larvae by regurgitation as well, and larvae destined to become queens are fed primarily by regurgitation. Most larvae share a common pollen store, however, and must compete for their share. This can result in size differences among the workers.

The queen continues to incubate the brood when she is not out foraging. The larvae pass quickly through the four instars, so in seven to fourteen days they are ready to pupate. Silk is released from the salivary glands as the larva spins around in its cell, making a cocoon. At this time, tissue blocking the rectum breaks down; accumulated larval feces are voided, then smeared on the walls of the cocoon, where they help form the structure. Because the feces contain the indigestible outer shells ("exines") of pollen grains, and because these pollen grains bear species-specific sculpturing, it is possible to reconstruct the entire larval diet of the bee by appropriate treatment and microscopic examination of the empty cocoon. The queen lays additional eggs on the sides of the larval clump or cocoons.

Pupation lasts about fourteen days. The first workers emerge from their cocoons about five weeks after the eggs were laid, although this period varies from as little as three weeks to as long as seven. The queen may cut the cocoon with her mandibles to help the young emerge. A newly emerged or "callow" bumblebee is silvery in color, with matted hair (Photograph 2-5, page 110). It cleans itself, drinks from the honeypot, and remains in the nest as its coat dries and wings harden over the course of several hours. In two to three days it displays its adult color pattern.

Once the first workers have emerged, the queen spends more time in the nest, laying eggs more frequently. When the worker force is sufficient, she remains within the nest. The synchrony of successive broods breaks down.

THE WORKER BEES

Worker bees are nonreproductive females (except, as mentioned, they sometimes lay unfertilized eggs that develop into males). Their roles are to construct the nest, regulate its temperature, feed the larvae, defend the colony, and forage for the colony. Shortly after emergence, the workers assume roles within the nest. They begin producing wax within two days and become involved in construction and modification of cells and storage vessels, sometimes bringing in additional nest material, and maintaining nest temperature and humidity. The temperature of the brood can be increased by muscular contractions, as previously described. Nest temperature can be lowered when bees mount the top of the nest and fan their wings to ventilate the nest. This behavior produces a rather loud, humming buzz, leading early naturalists to suppose that these bees were "trumpeters" rousing the colony to action.

The queen continues to lay eggs, and the colony grows outward and upward in layers as she attaches her new egg cells to old structures. As workers emerge, empty cocoons are modified with wax into storage containers for nectar and pollen (Photograph 2-6, page 110). Workers can produce new wax for construction, but they also tear down old structures and reuse wax. Many species construct a waxen roof over the colony to provide waterproofing and insulation. Sometimes this roof is torn down by day and rebuilt each night.

Nectar and pollen reserves are low compared to those of honeybees; they can generally sustain a colony for only a few inclement days. If nectar remains in the colony for any period of time, the water component evaporates, leaving a thick honey. Large colonies with many foragers sometimes collect so much nectar that they will cap some of their honeypots with wax until these reserves are needed.

Guard bees patrol the nest entrance and attempt to ward off intruders looking for a meal, or other bees seeking to usurp the colony. There is variation among bumblebee species in their levels of aggression toward intruders. If the colony is disturbed, the workers mount a defense and may sting intruders. If an individual is disturbed, she usually raises her middle legs in an aggressive posture. If the disturbance continues, she may roll onto her back with mandibles open and stinger visible.

Each bumblebee colony develops its own distinctive odor. If another bee with the wrong scent attempts to enter, it may be attacked. Other bumblebee queens, or *Psithyrus* queens, may attempt to take over a nest and its workforce to raise their own young. Initially these queens are attacked, bitten, and often stung to death. Several dead queens are sometimes found within a nest, and the reigning queen may not be the original foundress. If an interloper can survive the initial attacks, she may eventually be accepted by the workers. While fighting, worker bees may eject a watery liquid from the anus, or even regurgitate honey on invading bees so they become sticky and depart.

Young workers tend to remain in or close to the colony. The smallest bees may even be unable to fly and may spend their entire lives within the nest. Worker bees generally progress from nest chores to foraging; however, this progression is flexible, depending upon the needs of the colonies.

Foraging is strenuous. The wings of old foragers are tattered along the trailing edges, and their pile becomes thin and faded.

Workers can live as long as two months or even longer, depending on the type of activities they perform. Under poor conditions a worker's life span may be only two weeks. Bees staying within the nest live longer than foragers. In a study of *Bombus agrorum* (now known as *B. pascuorum*), only 71 percent of all eggs hatched, 73 percent of the larvae became pupae, and 90 percent of the pupae became adults (Brian 1951, 1952). Overall, 47 percent of the eggs survived to adulthood. Reported average life spans for workers are 13.2 days in *B. terricola* (Rodd, Plowright, and Owen 1980) and 30 days in *B. lucorum* (Müller, Shykoff, and Sutcliffe 1992). Worker mortality rates of 29 percent per five-day period have been recorded for *B. agrorum* (Brian 1952). The size of the workforce varies among species but rarely exceeds several hundred (Morse 1982). Overwintering colonies of *B. terrestris* in New Zealand and tropical bumblebees (such as *B. incarum*) that can forage throughout the year, however, may have colonies with several thousand workers (Alford 1975; Corbet, personal communication). In cooler, seasonal climates many species have a total workforce below 100. High-elevation and high-latitude colonies may be half that size.

Bumblebee colonies are cooperative units with distinct roles for queens and workers. Queens lay eggs and become dependent on workers to supply food. Workers typically forgo their own reproduction and perform tasks essential to development of a strong colony that can produce reproductive bees. Over the course of the summer the workforce grows strong. Ultimately there is a switch from worker production to the production of males and new queens. The sterile workers are essential in supplying and caring for the reproductive forms—the males and the new queens who are their brothers and sisters.

Reproductive Forms

The factors involved in the switch from worker production to reproductive production are not well understood, although this is under active investigation by firms that sell bumblebee colonies for commercial pollination. Early production of males seems to be common in artificially reared colonies, and this is highly undesirable for pollination. Even in natural situations, though, timing of male production is somewhat variable, and in some colonies males appear considerably earlier than new queens. Factors likely to play a role include adequate food, a sufficient workforce, worker bee–to–larva ratio, and seasonal cues. The emergence of reproductives should coincide among colonies of the same species to ensure mating.

When the old queen lays unfertilized eggs, they develop into males. After emerging, the young male bees remain in the nest for two to four days, during which time they may help with incubation. Once they leave the nest, however, they do not come back. They live for three to four weeks, foraging and seeking mates. Males spend the night resting on flowers, sometimes in large male aggregations. Patches of knapweed or thistle flowers are among the preferred sleeping sites.

In some species, whether a female larva develops into a queen or a worker appears to depend on the amount of food provided and the length of time spent in the larval stage. In honeybees, royal jelly or special food is provided to larvae destined to be queens, but in bumblebees, queen development seems to require only greater quantities of food.

In other species, the old queen seems to exert pheromonal control over the workers that feed the larvae. Therefore the old queen, through regulation of feeding regimes, determines when new queens will be produced. These tend to be pollen-storing species with large colonies and longer annual cycles. The queen often acts aggressively toward workers, butting, biting, and wrestling. Workers with more highly developed ovaries suffer the brunt of her aggression.

Once the old queen switches to producing reproductive forms, she does not revert to making workers. The developing queens spend a longer period in the larval stage than do workers. Upon emerging, a young queen seems to remain in the nest for some time, feeding on colony reserves and building up an abdominal fat body that will allow her to overwinter. Occasionally she will go out to forage and return to the nest. At about five days after emergence, a young queen may leave the nest to seek mates.

Males of different species have different techniques for finding females. Some have very large compound eyes, and they station themselves near a rock, a flower, or a patch of bare ground where they watch for young queens. A queen—or a flying object of similar size—elicits a chase. Some males wait at nest entrances for emerging queens. Others establish routes that they patrol, stopping regularly at certain spots along the way. These stops can involve a slow deliberate flight from base to tip of specific plants along the route. Or in some species, like the ones Darwin studied, males visit plants at a characteristic height, anywhere from 1 or 2 m above the ground to treetop level. Pheromones from the male mandibular gland are used to mark points along the route. Pheromones are species-specific in their effects, but their fragrance is often perceptible to humans if the male bumblebee is held in the hand.

Mating is rarely seen in the wild, but apparently takes place on the ground, among leaves, on flowers, or even in flight. Fertilized queens may return to the nest or begin searching for a winter hibernation site. A few reports indicate that young queens of some species (Alford 1975) occasionally produce a second summer brood.

After the production of reproductives, the number of workers diminishes and nest maintenance declines. Workers forage for themselves and eventually die. The old queen and the males die as well. Scavengers such as wax moths and beetle larvae destroy the old comb.

A young queen feeds until her fat body is well developed and then fills her crop with honey in preparation for hibernation. A large queen may store 200 mg of honey and contain 100 mg of fat (Alford 1975). Some species produce queens before the summer is over, and hibernation begins while flowers are still available, while others hibernate later in the season. Hibernation site preferences are also species-specific. Some species are known to hibernate in the vicinity of the parental nest, with many sisters in close proximity. Queens burrow 5 to 15 cm below the ground. As the temperature cools, they produce glycerol internally, which prevents ice crystals from forming in their tissues. (Glycerol production is common in insects and other organisms that overwinter in cold climates.) The queens remain underground until spring when the cycle begins again.

3

FORAGING BEHAVIOR

South winds jostle them—
Bumblebees come—
Hover—hesitate—
Drink, and are gone—

Butterflies pause
On their passage Cashmere—
I—softly plucking,
Present them here!

—EMILY DICKINSON

The foraging bee visits colorful flowers and serves as a vector for pollen. Because both the bees and the plants benefit, this relationship is considered a mutualistic one. It would be a mistake, however, to conclude that the bees and the plants share the same harmonious goal. Bright, fragrant flowers advertise themselves and solicit pollinators, for without them many plants cannot reproduce. The unwitting bee serves the flowers, but only as a by-product of fulfilling her own needs. The bee seeks nectar and pollen for herself and the colony. From her point of view, pollen exists to be fed to larvae, not delivered to stigmas; therefore, the interests of plant and pollinator conflict. Yet strong adaptations of both plant and pollinator are evidence of the importance of the relationship and of a long evolutionary history.

Bumblebee flowers tend to be brightly colored and visibly distinct from the background of green vegetation. Bees have good color vision, shifted toward the blue end of the spectrum compared to our own vision. They can perceive ultraviolet wavelengths that are invisible to human eyes. Although they have less sensitivity to longer wavelengths, leading to the frequent contention that "bees cannot see red," this is an overstatement. They can learn to recognize and remember both colors and patterns. Many flowers bear dots or stripes called "nectar guides," leading the bee to the source of the floral reward. These guides may be visible to us, or may be apparent only as UV patterns. Bee flowers are often fragrant as well, the fragrance attracting the bees and aiding in recognition. Most flowers produce nectar, a high-energy fuel whose sole purpose is to attract pollinators. Nectar rewards bees for their services and encourages their return. In some plants, however, pollen is the only food reward for pollinators.

Through all stages of the life cycle, bumblebees are dependent on a floral diet. Morphological and physiological adaptations to flower visiting are pronounced, as noted in Chapter 1: branched body hairs for collecting pollen, combs on their legs for grooming pollen, and corbiculae for transporting pollen. In flight they also bear an electrostatic charge that attracts pollen. The complex tongue is modified for sipping and lapping nectar; it is not a simple sucking tube like a butterfly's proboscis, but takes up nectar by sponging and sucking. The crop is modified into a honeystomach that can store nectar for transport back to the nest.

Some species of bees have short tongues and are restricted to visiting flowers with shallow corolla tubes (Table 1-1). Others have longer tongues that can probe flowers with deep corolla tubes to access larger nectar rewards unavailable to the majority of short-tongued insects. Bumblebee tongues range in length from about 6 to 18 mm. When we speak of "bumblebee flowers" we often refer to flowers with deep corollas, such as *Aconitum* (monkshood), *Delphinium* (larkspur), *Digitalis* (foxgloves), and *Pedicularis* (lousewort), all of which seem to be designed for long-tongued bumblebees. One long-tongued European species, *Bombus consobrinus*, has a close relationship with *Aconitum*, and this bee may visit little else if *Aconitum* is available. But bumblebees are typically generalists that visit a broad range of floral types. Within a community, short-tongued species tend to use different sets of flowers than long-tongued species. Yet, even within a colony, there is variation in tongue length, corresponding to variation in bee body size. A new forager will explore numerous flower species, gradually specializing on those that yield better rewards.

When nectar is inaccessible within long corolla tubes, several species of shorter-tongued bumblebees (Table 1-1) will bite holes in corollas, a behavior termed "nectar robbing" because the bee never contacts the reproductive parts of the flower (Inouye 1982). Other bees, including honeybees, are secondary nectar robbers that prefer to visit these nectar holes rather than attempting to probe the flower.

Much has been written about the foraging behavior of bumblebees, and bumblebees have been popular study organisms for testing optimal foraging theory (Morse 1982; Plowright and Laverty 1984). To present a rather simplistic summary, optimal foraging theory assumes that behaviors have evolved to maximize net energy intake per time spent during a foraging bout. We need to consider net energy gain (food intake minus energy expenditure) because an animal uses up energy during foraging as well as collecting energy in the form of food. Because food distribution is patchy and because some flowers are likely to be more rewarding than others, a forager is faced with behavioral decisions, such as how long to forage in a patch while the remaining energy reward declines. Traveling to a new patch consumes energy and time, so the greater rewards of a fresh patch must repay the travel costs of getting there. Worker bumblebees have been favored organisms for optimal foraging studies because they are assumed to have few other critical decisions to make while foraging for nectar. Unlike organisms that need to balance foraging activities with searching for mates, avoiding predators, or seeking out a balanced diet, nectar foragers are relatively free from these other constraints. In addition, although nectar provides small quantities of salts and minerals, it is primarily a sugar solution used for energy. In consequence, much research has been done on the energetics of bumblebee foraging for nectar. (Pollen collecting is a somewhat more complicated affair that has received much less attention, and is therefore an area in which amateurs could make original contributions.)

Large, complex flowers such as monkshood and foxglove often provide large nectar rewards. Individual florets of composites, or tiny flowers of many mint or clover plants, provide minute rewards. The tiny flowers are clustered together in great numbers, however, and the bee expends little energy crawling from one to the next. In a cost-benefit analysis, which flowers are most profitable may depend on a number of factors, including nectar volumes, nectar concentrations, the distances of flowers from the nest, the distances between flowers in a patch, the presence of competing bee species foraging in the area, a bee's previous experiences, and even the ambient temperature.

Why is ambient temperature of any significance in bee foraging behavior? Because it enters into the energy balance ledger. Most insects simply become inactive at unfavorable temperatures; bumblebees do not. They have a large volume–to–surface area ratio and are well insulated. They can be seen foraging under colder (–3.6°C; Heinrich 1979) and more extreme conditions than most other bees. In addition, they have been described foraging during snowfall, when frost is on the ground, and even at night during a full moon. Insects' flight muscles must be warm in order to function. Most bees cannot fly when the ambient temperature is lower than 16°C (Heinrich 1979). For bumblebees thoracic muscle temperature is generally between 30° and 40°C (Prys-Jones and Corbet 1991) during flight.

While the bee is flying, heat is generated by contraction of the flight muscles. In flight a bumblebee's metabolic rate is about twice that of a hummingbird per unit body weight, and its wings beat about two hundred times per second (Heinrich 1979). When the bee stops, however, the thoracic temperature begins dropping toward the ambient temperature. If it falls below 27°C, the bee cannot fly. But unlike most insects, bumblebees have two processes that allow them to regulate thoracic temperature. One involves muscular thermogenesis, a process in which the thoracic muscles are used to generate heat rather than produce motion. During muscular thermogenesis the bee's thoracic muscles are uncoupled from the wings, and antagonistic muscles are contracted, generating heat and tension with minimal movement. Simultaneous pumping motion of the abdomen serves to aerate the thoracic muscles (Heinrich 1993). The process is energy-consuming but permits bumblebees to forage at low temperatures when competitors may be absent and nectar levels in flowers high. (Recall that incubating queens also use thermogenesis to keep eggs and larvae at desirable temperatures.) In addition, bumblebees can conserve energy by visiting rewarding flowers that are clustered so that the bees can walk from flower to flower. Walking demands less energy than flight. By using a very small thermocouple-type thermometer, it can easily be shown that bees allow their thoracic temperatures to drop while working on a large composite flower head. They actively elevate their temperatures before leaving for the next bloom.

There is some debate about how far a bee will travel from its nest to collect food. The longer the flight distance, the more energy-consuming the flight, so optimal foraging theory suggests that bees should minimize flight distances. Given a limited capacity of the honeystomach or pollen basket, and that the bee must return to the nest, a longer flight uses up time that could be spent collecting food. Much of the bee literature gives the sense that bees forage close to the nest in order to keep the cost-benefit ratio of foraging low. It is difficult to follow bees back to the nest, however, and actual foraging distances from the nest are not well documented.

There is clear evidence of bees returning to the same patches of flowers on different foraging bouts and over the course of several days, but how close these patches are to the nest has long been a matter of speculation. Additional knowledge about foraging distances would be valuable for managing bumblebees for crop pollination. Knowledge of foraging distances is also important for understanding pollen flow, especially when developing conservation plans for endangered species (Osborne et al. 1999).

In a recent review of this issue, Dramstad (1996) marked all the foraging bees from several different nests and attempted to determine their foraging ranges. Despite abundant resources of preferred floral species and the presence of other bees in the area, few marked bees were seen foraging close to the nest. Observers noted high rates of departure and return of marked bees at the nest, indicating that the marked bees were out foraging even though they were not in the adjacent fields. R. Chris Plowright noted similar patterns in New Brunswick, Canada (personal communication). In contrast, when bees were marked while foraging in a patch of flowers, rates of reobservation within the patch were high. Dramstad concluded that foraging close to the nest is rare.

Osborne et al. (1999) fitted bumblebees with tiny radar transponders and followed their movements from the nest to foraging sites in crop fields. They confirmed that foraging bumblebees do not minimize flight distances from the nest when choosing floral patches, and that the bees do tend to be patch-constant. By contrast, Thomson, Peterson, and Harder (1987) found a number of *Bombus affinis* workers (including the famous Yellow mentioned in the foreword) foraging within 40 m of their nest box. What might explain the difference? In Thomson, Peterson, and Harder's study, a large number of wild bees had previously been caught and marked in the area. Because the trauma of marking might make some bees leave a feeding area, the marking program may have created a competitive vacuum near the *affinis* nest that made it particularly advantageous for these bees to stay near home.

We know very little about how a bee selects a patch or patches in which to concentrate her foraging efforts. It seems likely that sampling is involved; a new forager probably samples flowers near the nest. If they are rewarding, she may settle down to use that patch for days to come. If those flowers have been drained by other bees, however, she will probably range farther afield. Bees commonly fly several hundred meters to preferred forage patches and then switch to traveling short distances between flowers. That is, they may well be minimizing flight distances within patches, as optimal foraging theory suggests, but different rules may apply at the larger scale of patch-choice decisions. The willingness of bumblebees to range widely has at least two important implications: first, the bees working in a local area are rather unlikely to be hive-mates, so we would not expect them to forage cooperatively; second, agricultural use of bumblebee colonies as pollinators of field crops may be difficult, especially if there are alternative flower species growing in the vicinity. Additional research on this topic would be valuable.

Once within a patch, individual bumblebees face decisions about which flower species to visit. Some species are simply unattractive by virtue of having too little reward for these large bees, or because their rewards are inaccessible. Frequently, however, a local area offers several flower species that are all suitable fodder for bumblebees. Although all these species of plants may be visited by a particular species of bumblebee, individual bees frequently concentrate their visits on a single plant species. This behavior, termed "flower constancy," is probably the oldest recorded aspect of bee behavior, as Aristotle mentioned it. Flower constancy is highly developed in certain solitary bees and honeybees, but in bumblebees it is usually manifested as a partial, rather than absolute, preference for one flower type. Heinrich (1976) interpreted this as a tendency for bumblebees to choose one flower species for bulk foraging while sampling from two or three other species, a pattern he labeled "majoring" and "minoring."

Constancy is a difficult phenomenon to explain, particularly in terms of models of optimal diet (Waser 1986). When equally rewarding flowers are interspersed in a meadow, why should a bee skip over one kind? Doing so will increase flight costs without providing any food intake. Various authors, including Darwin, have proposed mechanisms by which specialization promotes efficiency. The prevailing current view, reviewed by Chittka, Thomson, and Waser (1999), is that constancy probably arises from neurological constraints on learning, memory, and the motor patterns needed to work different flowers effectively. Bees learn to recognize the shape, color, and fragrance of rewarding flowers, and learn about the time when floral rewards are present (Michener 1974). They seem to be born with some very basic flower-handling skills; for example, they react to a flower-scented tube by putting their proboscis down it. They are clumsy, however, at more elaborate tasks. With practice a bumblebee becomes more efficient at handling flowers of a given species, spending less time to extract the same reward. Complex flowers like monkshood (*Aconitum*) or turtlehead (*Chelone*) require specialized handling to locate and extract a hidden nectar reward. Some naive bumblebees visiting monkshood may visit several flowers without success and then give up trying, perhaps for life. Others may get lucky on their first few tries, continue to refine their handling skills, and perhaps specialize on these uniquely complex flowers (Laverty and Plowright 1988). Although Chittka, Thomson, and Waser (1999) conclude that bees are not forced into flower-constant behavior by the inability of their long-term memories to contain multiple sets of flower-handling instructions, they argue that the time needed to "upload" those instructions into short-term or working memory may slow down foraging. They also point out that learning one pattern can interfere with learning a second pattern, and that learning new flowers generally reduces foraging efficiency, at least in the short term. There are thus numerous ways in which neural constraints may favor some degree of constancy. More experimental work with bumblebees will help resolve the picture.

Although forsaking the major forage species occasionally to minor on another species incurs short-term costs, this foraging mode may increase the lifetime efficiency of an inconstant bumblebee by allowing the bee to track changes in the availability of different plant species. The plant community is not static. A forager's life span may not coincide with the flowering phenology of a particular plant, and the bees themselves are depleting floral rewards. Therefore, many foragers will have to switch food plants at some point. Bees of the same colony often major and minor on different plants, allowing the colony to take advantage of a variety of resources. Colony preferences are in part regulated by the presence of competitive foraging species. Inouye (1978) demonstrated that several bee species in an area are likely to divide the floral resources based on tongue length and corresponding corolla tube length. But if one bee species is removed from the area, there is a shift in the distribution of the other bee species over to the available floral resources.

While in a patch of flowers, a bumblebee tends to maintain a directional movement, which minimizes the chance of revisiting an emptied flower (Pyke and Cartar 1992). Bumblebees often reject flowers recently visited by other bumblebees, although they do not reject flowers from which nectar has been removed artificially (Goulson, Hawson, and Stout 1998). This suggests that bees are scent-marking flowers. Other possible mechanisms for detection of nectar include scent emanating from the nectar itself, humidity gradients around the flower, and the visual presence of nectar. (They can also detect the presence of pollen visually.) Even the human nose can distinguish nectar-drained from nectar-rich clover heads. Apparently bumblebees can also mark flowers that are especially rewarding, a behavior that promotes probing by other bees. When floral rewards are high, there is a greater tendency for the bees to revisit previously emptied flowers (Heinrich 1979). Might this be an early example of a bee tuning to a short intervisit interval in response to a high secretion rate? Might it be expressed and interpreted differently in light of what is now known about scent-marking?

Bumblebees visiting *Aralia hispida* seem to pay relatively little attention to scents. Rather, they determine whether a flower is empty or not mostly by sampling it. But they do use the state of one flower (drained or full) to predict the state of others. Thomson, Maddison, and Plowright (1982) gave free-foraging bees a choice of two inflorescences, each of which contained twelve open flowers arranged in a circle. One inflorescence was drained; the other was enriched. Bees did not discriminate between the two inflorescences on their first approach. When they encountered the drained inflorescence first, they typically visited two flowers, then left without examining the enriched inflorescence. When they chose the enriched inflorescence first, they worked systematically around the circle, hitting about fourteen flowers; then, almost invariably, they flew to the adjacent drained inflorescence, where they visited four to five flowers. These data suggest that bees were using a "departure rule" that said, in effect, "Leave an inflorescence after getting two empties in a row." It also appears that bees expected nectar crops to be patchy; that is, if they encountered a drained inflorescence, they assumed that the adjacent one was empty, too. Finally, it appears that if they encountered an empty inflorescence when they were expecting a full one, they reacted in "disbelief," sampling more empty flowers before giving up.

Bumblebees also show informative behaviors on vertical inflorescences of certain plants. An influential paper by Pyke (1978a) suggested the following story. Bees tend to visit the lowest flowers first and move up the stem, leaving before reaching the top. In some of these plants, flowers open sequentially from bottom to top. Each flower first enters a male phase during which it sheds its pollen but is unable to receive pollen. Later, after its own pollen is gone, it becomes receptive as a female, and the rate of nectar production goes up. Therefore, the lowest flowers are in the receptive female stage and typically contain more nectar. With such a pattern of nectar, a result from optimal foraging theory called the "marginal value theorem" predicts not only that bees should start at the bottom but also that they should leave before reaching the top flower, if they can increase their intake by flying to the richer bottom flowers of another inflorescence. This means that bumblebees arriving from other plants may pollinate the female flowers before visiting the male-phase flowers on the same stalk, a mechanism that promotes outcrossing of the plant. Pyke (1978a) speculated that the plants were manipulating the nectar gradient from bottom to top in order to make optimally foraging bees go upward. Elegant later experiments with artificial vertical inflorescences revealed that bumblebees would still go upward even when the gradient was reversed; flying upward simply seems to be easier for an animal whose eyes and antennae are oriented facing up. Bees did adjust their starting points and departure points on the artificial inflorescences in ways consistent with saving energy, however (Waddington and Heinrich 1979).

After landing on a flower, a bumblebee foraging specifically for pollen may crawl over the anthers and subsequently groom the pollen into its corbiculae, or actively collect the pollen with legs and mandibles. On plants with poricidal anthers such as tomatoes and nightshades, the bumblebee grasps the anthers in its mandibles and hangs from the flower while vibrating its wings, creating a shower of pollen. Although it seems improbable, much of the released pollen sticks to the bee's pile by electrostatic attraction. The same puffs of pollen can be produced by vibrating the anthers of these flowers with a musical tuning fork. Bumblebees can carry 20 percent of their body weight in pollen within the corbiculae. Pollen collection is stimulated by the presence of a brood in the nest and diminishes if larvae are removed from the nest (Free 1987).

Bumblebees can collect pollen and nectar on the same foraging bout or specialize on one resource. Very commonly, one sees a bee probing flowers actively for nectar without showing obvious behaviors directed at pollen collecting; the bee is nevertheless acquiring pollen loads more or less passively. Smaller foragers tend to gather nectar only, but there is much individual variation. Nectar foragers return to the nest carrying from 20 to 100 percent of their own body weight in nectar (Heinrich 1979). The nectar is regurgitated into wax storage pots in the hive, and the bumblebee leaves within minutes for another load. Nectar foraging may cease temporarily when all pots are full (Alford 1975). Bumblebees have long been thought to lack any mechanism like the famous "waggle dance" of the honeybee for recruiting other colony members to a favorable food source, but recent experiments by Dornhaus and Chittka (1999) suggest that successful returning bumblebee workers do convey some information to others by the floral scents they carry and by their excited movements (more a "slam dance" than a waggle). This too is a new area where investigation by amateurs may bring new insights.

Pollen and nectar are the essential foods required by bumblebees. Nonetheless, they have also been known to collect sap from trees, visit extrafloral nectaries, and visit aphids to gather honeydew. Herrera (1990) reports bumblebees feeding on carrion, bird droppings, urine, and feces. He suggests that their high nitrogen content attracted the bees.

Studies of marked bumblebees have shown that some bees limit their foraging to a restricted set of plants and repeatedly visit the same plants at fairly regular intervals. This behavior, known as "traplining," may allow bees to incorporate rewarding plants in a circuit, thus minimizing search time while allowing time for nectar to replenish between visits. Trapline foragers sample new flowers often enough that circuits change somewhat over the course of several days as new plants are incorporated and plants that are no longer rewarding are dropped from the circuit. In arrays of the plant *Penstemon strictus*, regular trapliners return to their plants at about seven-minute intervals, and four or five workers may account for the majority of the hundreds of visits that a plant receives during a day. These regular visitors appear to gain an advantage over casual, nontraplining visitors because they are better at selecting flowers that have not recently been visited (Williams and Thomson 1998).

4

PREDATORS AND PARASITES

When Roses cease to bloom, Sir,
And Violets are done—
When Bumblebees in solemn flight
Have passed beyond the Sun—
The hand that paused to gather
Upon this Summer's day
Will idle lie—in Auburn—
Then take my flower—pray!

—EMILY DICKINSON

Bumblebees are plagued by a number of predators and parasites, and their nests are infested with freeloaders (Alford 1975; Morse 1982). Morse (1982) reports that bumblebee nests may contain fifty to sixty insect species from as many as twelve different orders. Some of these insects simply use the nest for shelter, whereas others feed on nest materials, the bee brood, or other stages of the bee life cycle. Interactions between bees and their predators and parasites can be interesting, and the impacts of these organisms on bumblebee population fluctuations warrant further study.

Parasites can have dramatic effects on bumblebee populations and may be very significant in regulating population size. Parasites can also affect the behavior of bees in ways that help ensure parasite transmission (see "Diptera"). On a much longer time scale, parasites have probably been important in the evolution of sociality in insects. Some parasites are known to promote congregation of individuals, which of course aids in parasite transmission. Larger social groups often harbor more parasites and may benefit from cooperative defensive behaviors. Parasitic infection can also reduce the fecundity of individuals, so natural selection may favor behaviors by which parasitized bees help their close relatives reproduce, thus ensuring the transmission into the next generation of the genes they share. This mechanism has the potential to favor cooperative behavior and kin selection (Schmid-Hempel 1998). Many interesting questions remain concerning the proximate effects of parasites on individual behavior and population dynamics. Studies in this area are likely to further our understanding of ultimate evolutionary roles played by parasites as well. For more detailed information on the life cycles of bee parasites, as well as a thorough review of these evolutionary issues, see Schmid-Hempel's book *Parasites in Social Insects*.

The following is a taxonomic catalog of some of the most important natural enemies of bumblebees.

HYMENOPTERA

Bombus

Some bumblebees exploit other bumblebees. *Bombus* queens that emerge late, have their nests destroyed, or are otherwise unable to start a nest will sometimes appropriate the nests of other bumblebees and behave as social parasites. Queen replacement, known as "supercedure," may occur several times within the same nest, as evidenced by the presence of up to twenty dead queens in a single nest (Sladen 1912). Usually a queen attempts to take over a nest of the same species. Supercedure of nests of other species is said to occur most commonly within the same subgenus, but has been documented between subgenera as well. If the homeless queen manages to penetrate nest defenses, she eventually engages in mortal combat with the resident queen. If the new queen wins, she begins laying her own eggs and permits the resident brood to develop and serve as her workforce.

Bombus fervidus and *B. rufocinctus* queens are known to usurp nests, as are *B. affinis* queens, who regularly invade colonies of *B. terricola*. Supercedure is routine in the Arctic, where *B. hyperboreus* queens habitually take over the nests of *B. polaris* (Michener 1974). In the short Arctic summer, *B. hyperboreus* workers are never produced and the queen depends entirely on *B. polaris* workers to raise her reproductive offspring. Farther south, where the summer is longer, *B. hyperboreus* workers are produced and the species exhibits more typical *Bombus* behavior.

Psithyrus

Although *Bombus* queens may be opportunistic social parasites, *Psithyrus* bees specialize in the parasitic lifestyle. *Psithyrus* is a large cuckoo bee, related to and similar in appearance to *Bombus*. In fact, in the most recent taxonomic treatment (P. H. Williams 1998), *Psithyrus* has been subsumed under *Bombus*, but we retain the old distinction. On close inspection, *Psithyrus* exhibits those features common to all cuckoo bees or "inquilines," bees that lay their eggs in others' nests. There is no worker caste, only reproductive females and males. The host species provides workers that feed the *Psithyrus* queen and raise her offspring.

Psithyrus females lack corbiculae, the depressions on the hind leg used for carrying pollen. Instead the hind tibia is convex and hairy. A *Psithyrus* queen has a strong stinger and a long, recurved abdomen covered with a heavy cuticle. These structures protect her from the defensive stings of bumblebees guarding the nest she attempts to conquer. The black cuticle shows through the sparse hair on the *Psithyrus* abdomen.

A *Psithyrus* female emerges from her subterranean burrow later in the spring than does *Bombus* and then spends her time feeding on nectar and pollen. Her flight is slower than that of a true bumblebee. Once her ovaries develop, she begins searching for a bumblebee nest. Olfactory cues are likely to be involved in nest discovery. Ideally the *Psithyrus* queen should invade a nest when the bumblebee workforce is large enough to raise her brood but small enough so that she can overpower nest defenses. Some *Psithyrus* queens hide within the *Bombus* nest for several days, acquiring the nest smell and allowing workers to become used to their presence. Other *Psithyrus* queens are more aggressive and enter the nest openly. Bumblebee workers try to sting such an invader and drive her off, but her thick cuticle and strong jaws often protect her. She may kill several workers or may herself be killed in the process. If she succeeds in establishing herself in the nest, she sometimes kills the queen and destroys eggs and larvae present in the nest. Alternatively she may coexist with the resident queen for many weeks, but in this situation the *Bombus* queen becomes subdued and any eggs she lays are destroyed.

The *Psithyrus* female is unable to make wax, but she manipulates wax present in the nest and creates cells for her own eggs. When the eggs hatch, the bumblebee workers feed and care for the *Psithyrus* larvae.

Although the basic biology of *Psithyrus* bees is known, much remains to be learned about their evolution and ecology. The group appears to be monophyletic, contrary to some early suggestions that social parasites arose independently from several lineages within the genus *Bombus*. The factors regulating *Psithyrus* populations are poorly known. The magnitude of their effect on *Bombus* colonies varies among regions but may be an important factor affecting *Bombus* population sizes and population oscillations.

Beewolves

Sphecid wasps in the genus *Philanthus* hunt bees and other wasps to provision their nests with larval food. These wasps, dubbed "beewolves" by Niko Tinbergen (Evans and O'Neill 1988), have fascinated behavioral biologists because of their complex and flexible behaviors. *P. bicinctus*, the bumblebee-wolf, is the largest beewolf in North America, with localized populations occurring in the Rocky Mountains from Montana to Utah at elevations from 2,000 to 2,800 m. Males average 17 mm in length and bear typical wasp color patterns of alternating black and yellow. Females average

22 mm in length and have black abdomens with a single orange band followed by a single yellow band at the base of the abdomen (Evans and O'Neill 1988).

Male beewolves are territorial, incorporating three to twenty nests per territory. A male has one or more perches, such as prominent rocks or sticks with little surrounding vegetation. He periodically leaves his perch to scent-mark his territory, smearing secretions from the mandibular glands along the entire length of tall blades of grass. He also leaves his perch to investigate large insects flying near. Conspecifics are grabbed in midair and wrestled to the ground. If the intruder is a male, fighting and biting continue on the ground; if a female, copulation is attempted.

Female beewolves nest in loose aggregations, using the same site for as long as thirty years (Evans and O'Neill 1988). With her mandibles and front legs, a female digs her nest in loose soil. A mound of soil, 15–21 cm in diameter, is found near the tunnel entrance. The tunnel enters the ground at an oblique angle and extends 50–90 cm before leveling to a somewhat more horizontal position, albeit with meandering turns and undulations. Shorter tunnels, 4–10 cm long, branch off the semihorizontal portion and lead to brood cells. Each cell is provisioned with about five bumblebees. The bees are captured while feeding on flowers and paralyzed by a sting from the female wasp. The effect on the bumblebee population can be significant: a population of 200 female wasps with an average of eight cells per nest can remove 7,500 bumblebees (Gwynne 1981). In years with low numbers of bumblebees, the beewolves are able to switch to smaller, though less-preferred, bee and wasp species.

Other hymenopterans can have negative effects on bumblebee colonies. Ants attack bumblebee nests whenever possible and can destroy colonies that have been exposed for field observation. Several types of wasps may parasitize bee broods (*Melittobia* spp., Eulophidae) or have predatory larvae that may consume bee broods (*Mutilla europaea*, Mutillidae; Morse 1982).

Wax Moths

Several kinds of moths breed in bumblebee nests. Many of them are harmless, but others are devastating. One of the most harmful moths is the introduced European wax moth, *Aphomia sociella* (Pyralidae). *Aphomia* caterpillars eat the bumblebee comb and food stores, and ultimately destroy the colony. As many as one hundred gray-green or gray-yellow caterpillars may occupy a single nest. These larvae produce galleries made of a tough silk throughout the nest. They move through the galleries, eating nest debris, stored food, and bumblebee larvae. Ultimately they exit the nest to spin cocoons and overwinter, leaving behind masses of tough silk throughout the colony (Prys-Jones and Corbet 1991). Adults, which emerge late in the summer, have a wingspread of 30–35 mm and are white or pale yellow with brown markings. The American wax moth, *Vitula edmandsii* (Pyralidae), feeds on wax, pollen, and nest debris without destroying the brood. Infected colonies may continue to thrive. At the end of the season, when the colony fails for other reasons, these moths may destroy the remains of the comb.

Mites

The varroa and tracheal mites (*Varroa jacobsoni, Acarapis woodi*), which have ravaged North American honeybee colonies in the 1990s, do not affect bumblebees. But there are other species of both tracheal mites (*Bombacarus buchneri*) and hemolymph feeders (*Scutacarus acarorum*) that parasitize bumblebees. Several other species of mites that associate with bumblebees have quite interesting behaviors. Some mites, such as *Tyrophagus* and *Parasitellus*, are phoretic, that is, they disperse by hitchhiking on foraging bees. When the bumblebee lands on a flower, the mite defects and waits for a ride to carry it to its new home. Upon close examination, one can often detect several species of mites on an individual bee, particularly if that bee is a queen. Most of the mites associated with bumblebees are nest commensals, eating nest debris, bee feces, or other mites that live in the nest (Morse 1982).

Beetles

Some beetles also consort with bumblebees, either as ectoparasites or as relatively harmless scavengers of nest debris. Silken fungus beetles (*Antherophagus*, Cryptophagidae) sit on a flower with open jaws, waiting to grab the leg, tongue, or antennae of a foraging bee (Plath 1934). The beetle dismounts upon reaching the bee nest, where it is likely to find many others of its kind, both adults and larvae. If a bumblebee arrives back at the nest with her tongue uncharacteristically extended, it is most likely because one of these phoretic beetles has clamped onto her proboscis during a flower probe.

Diptera

Several types of flies interact with bumblebees (Photographs 4-1 to 4-2, page 111). One group that includes bumblebee mimics is the robber fly family (Asilidae). Asilids prey on adult bees. *Brachycoma* spp. (Tachinidae) larvae feed on bee pupae within the nest. Several other fly species, such as *Fannia canicularis* (Anthomyiidae), lay eggs in bumblebee nests, and their larvae eat bee excrement. *Volucella bombylans* (Syrphidae), another bumblebee mimic, impersonates a bumblebee in size and color. When caught in a net, it buzzes like a bee. This mimic also lays its eggs in bumblebee nests, where its larvae are generally harmless scavengers. (But at least one species in the genus [*V. bombycolans*] is known to attack the brood [Morse 1982].)

Not all dipteran nest associates are so benign. Conopid flies (*Sicus* and *Physocephala*) target foraging bees. They may attack a bee on the flower, or wait for a victim to approach, then take off and attack the bee in flight (Corbet, personal communication). The female conopid deposits an egg through the bee's intersegmental membrane and into its abdomen. The egg hatches within the bee and progresses through three larval instars, killing its host late in the third instar. Larvae consume hemolymph and abdominal organs and grow to fill the entire abdomen. The fly pupates within the dead host's abdomen and emerges as an adult the following summer. Conopid infestation rates are quite variable, but may affect as much as 70 percent of a colony and decrease individual bees' life spans by 50 percent (Schmid-Hempel and Durrer 1991).

The effects of parasites on bee behavior, colony development, and colony success are beginning to receive attention. Conopid parasites clearly affect host behavior (C. Müller 1994). Host bees become torpid more frequently than unparasitized individuals and switch to foraging on flowers with shorter corolla tubes. Parasitized bees stay out of the nest for long periods, often not returning to the nest at night and perhaps abandoning the nest completely.

The conopid fly must pupate and overwinter wherever its host dies. Parasitism induces worker bees to dig 2–10 cm into the soil before dying underground. In experimental studies (C. Müller 1994), bumblebee carcasses left on the ground surface suffered predation and hyperparasitism, but those buried in the soil suffered less damage. In addition, bees recovered from underground showed fewer signs of decay than those on the surface. Parasites emerging from buried bees were larger and had fewer wing deformities, differences that are likely related to temperature fluctuations during development. Thus the altered behavior of the parasitized bee increases parasite fitness.

Parasitism by conopids can affect colony food stores by reducing the bees' ability to acquire resources. If parasitism rates are high, one expects reduced growth rates and reproductive success as well as consequences for plants requiring bumblebee pollinators. Bumblebee species that appear later in the summer are more susceptible to parasitism, and it has been suggested that parasitism is important in bee phenology (Schmid-Hempel et al. 1990). Because parasitized bees are likely to abandon the nest and remain in the field, studies of foraging economics of bees in the field may be affected by disrupted behavior patterns.

PROTISTS

The protozoan parasite *Nosema bombi* inhabits the gut and Malpighian tubules of bumblebees. Its near relative, *N. apis*, causes serious problems in honeybee colonies. *Nosema* infection so weakens a bee that it cannot fly. We understand that accidental infection by *Nosema* caused the recent collapse of commercial production of the western *Bombus occidentalis* in the United States. In consequence, the eastern species *B. impatiens* has been shipped to the West, where it is not native. Conservationists fear that such transcontinental movements will spread diseases further.

Crithidia bombi, an intestinal trypanosome parasite of bumblebees, may exert important effects on the social behavior of *Bombus* colonies (Shykoff and Schmid-Hempel 1991). This parasite is spread by ingestion of *Crithidia* cells from the feces of infected bees. Because bumblebee colonies are annual, *Crithidia* are probably present within some young queens who overwinter and then transmit the parasites to their developing colonies the following summer.

In mature bumblebee colonies, it is not uncommon for workers' ovaries to develop and for workers to produce male eggs. When workers lay eggs, there is aggression and conflict between the queen and workers. Infestation by *Crithidia* delays ovarian development in workers (Shykoff and Schmid-Hempel 1991). The implications of this delay are that a higher percentage of the colony's males are produced by the queen, which should reduce aggressive interactions between the queen and workers. The workers may continue brood care and foraging activities, resulting in the production of many large queens that can become infected, allowing winter persistence of the parasite. Production of male bees is not important to the spread of the parasite, so selection should favor parasites that promote new queen production. Because parasites promote cooperation among queens and workers, Shykoff and Schmid-Hempel (1991) suggest that through ovarian suppression, parasites may have played a part in the development of eusociality.

NEMATODES

The nematode parasite *Sphaerularia bombi* enters the bodies of young queens hibernating in the soil. As the female nematode develops within her host, her reproductive organs hypertrophy, becoming far larger than the rest of her body. This improbable feat requires that the ovaries be everted outside the body. Eggs are released into the host's hemocoel, the internal, fluid-filled cavity that contains the organs. Early larval instars develop within the egg. As many as 100,000 third-instar larvae, each about 1 mm long, emerge from their eggs and swim in the hemolymph (Alford 1975). Eventually they enter the digestive and reproductive tracts of the bee and make their way out of the host. The larvae mature and mate in the soil. Fertilized females seek out new hibernating queens in late summer.

Infestation prevents development of the young queen's ovaries and influences her behavior. Rather than initiating a colony, the young queen returns to the hibernation area, flying low and clumsily. She digs in the soil or crawls under leaf litter. The larvae emerge from the female and enter the soil in the hibernation area.

VERTEBRATE PREDATORS

Although vertebrates do not specialize on bumblebees, bees or their brood may be eaten by a variety of mammals, including mice, shrews, moles, voles, skunks, weasels, foxes, badgers, and bears. Birds such as shrikes and jays eat bumblebees as well.

5

BUMBLEBEE CONSERVATION

Bees stopped on the rock
and rubbed their headparts and wings
rested then flew on:
ants ran over the whitish greenish reddish
plants that grow flat on rocks
and people never see
because nothing should grow on rocks:
I looked out over the lake
and beyond to the hills and trees
and nothing was moving
so I looked closely
along the lakeside
under the old leaves of rushes
and around clumps of drygrass
and life was everywhere
so I went on sometimes whistling

—A. R. AMMONS, "Bees Stopped"

Declines in the abundance of pollinators have been documented on every continent but Antarctica. The potential consequences of pollinator declines are so extensive that some ecologists foresee an impending pollination crisis (Buchmann and Nabhan 1996; Kearns, Inouye, and Waser 1998). The majority of flowering plants require pollinators to produce fruits and seeds. The seeds resulting from pollination represent future generations of plants. Seeds, fruits, and plants represent the primary productivity of terrestrial ecosystems, forming the base of the food chain that supports all other life. Therefore pollinator declines have the potential to affect entire communities. Although many important plants are wind-pollinated or can set seed without pollination, communities dominated by these species would be unnatural and imbalanced in many ways. Loss of "ecosystem services" such as pollination has indirect and complex effects, resulting in unhealthy ecosystems.

Loss of pollinators could create both economic and conservation repercussions through declines in biodiversity and agricultural productivity.

The economic value associated with pollination of the world's crop plants has been estimated at $200 billion per year, with U.S. crop pollination valued at $20 billion to $40 billion per year (K. W. Richards 1993). Production of about one-third of the food people eat depends directly or indirectly on bee pollination (O'Toole 1993; P. W. Williams 1995).

In the United States the pollination services of bees other than the honeybee are valued at up to $6.7 billion per year (Nabhan and Buchmann 1997). The extent to which wild pollinators contribute to crop pollination has often been underestimated because wild pollinators may be insufficient in number to adequately service a crop without the help of domesticated honeybees. Destruction of wild pollinators by pesticides has sometimes revealed the significance of their contributions (Kearns, Inouye, and Waser 1998; Kevan 1975a).

Of the twenty thousand to thirty thousand bee species (Neff and Simpson 1993), most are obligate flower visitors. About two-thirds of these have been named and described, and only a small percentage have been studied rigorously. An unknown number of species will become extinct before receiving more than cursory attention (Tepedino 1979). Even in Europe, where bees have received more study than in many areas, there is still uncertainty about the number of species, with estimates ranging from 2,500 to 4,500 (C. S. Williams 1995).

Bumblebees are among the best studied of bees. They are important pollinators for a large number of plant species. Few other insects are large enough to manipulate flowers in the same manner, and many of our large, showy, nectar-rich flowers (delphiniums, monkshoods, penstemons, foxgloves, primroses) appear to have evolved in conjunction with bumblebee pollinators. Less specialized flowers that may be pollinated by a variety of pollinators are also often efficiently pollinated by bumblebees (willow flowers, wild roses, blackberries, geraniums, various composites). Bumblebees also service some crop plants; they are more effective than honeybees at pollinating several of these, including blueberries, cranberries, raspberries, tomatoes, red clover, and field beans.

Although bumblebee behavior and ecology are well known, their population dynamics are poorly understood. The same is true for almost all wild insects except certain pest species. Even so, it is clear that some species of bumblebees are in decline in many parts of the world. Recognition of these declines has resulted in protected status for bumblebees in Czechoslovakia, Poland, and Germany. Thirty-five species of *Bombus* are listed in the European Red Data List of species in need of conservation (Day 1991). Most bee declines can be attributed to habitat alteration. Development, urbanization, mechanized agriculture, and intensive grazing all alter the landscape, decreasing the habitat suitable for nesting sites and altering and reducing the floral variety available for bee forage. Although garden flowers can be important food sources for bees in urbanized habitats, many garden flowers have been bred for showiness only, and some lack nectar or pollen. As landscapes change, native plants are increasingly relegated to fragmented populations that are too small to attract or support pollinators. The likely consequences are increased inbreeding and loss of genetic diversity in already distressed plant species. The interaction of these effects on plants and pollinators can result in a spiral of decline.

AGRICULTURE

In general, bee declines receive little notice unless there is a negative effect on agricultural production. When crop yield or quality suffers in a way that suggests insufficient pollination, the nearly universal agricultural "solution" is to bring hives of honeybees to the crop. In many cases, this is extremely effective, for honeybees are generalists that are willing to visit many different species, most of which they pollinate reasonably well. What makes them almost unchallenged in agriculture, however, is the huge size of their colonies, coupled with a well-developed technology for producing, maintaining, and transporting those colonies. Their transportability is key; the bees can be brought to a crop exactly when needed. When the bloom is over, they can be taken away so that growers can resume pesticide treatments and other practices that would be prejudicial to the health of bees that had to nest in the area. Growers with recourse to honeybees can also get away with cultivating their land up to road edges, leaving no hedgerows or set-aside land for bee nesting. Although these techniques may maximize short-term profitability, they depend absolutely on a reliable supply of honeybees. But recent epidemics of mite diseases in Europe and the United States have greatly reduced honeybee numbers. In the northeastern United States, for example, feral (unmanaged) colonies are thought to have been nearly wiped out in the mid-1990s. Furthermore, many amateur beekeepers have abandoned the difficult task of keeping productive hives. Although professionals seem able to stay in business by careful monitoring and treatment, the decline in honeybee numbers has drawn growers' attention to the great desirability of maintaining wild pollinators for insurance.

Alternative pollinators can play roles in agriculture far beyond serving as "backup" for honeybees. There are some crops for which honeybees are not a good solution, regardless of how plentiful they are. One such is alfalfa, a very important forage plant for cattle. Alfalfa seed production requires insect pollination, which honeybees perform rather poorly. A solitary species, the alfalfa leafcutter bee (*Megachile rotundata*), has been developed as a superior alternative pollinator; most alfalfa-seed growers now either grow or buy these bees to produce their crops. On a per-flower-visit basis, bumblebees are also superior pollinators of alfalfa and other forage crops such as red clover, as well as some valuable fruit and nut crops such as blueberries, cranberries, and almonds. The problem usually lies in getting enough of those excellent visits. Although various attempts have been made to deploy bumblebee colonies to pollinate field crops, none has yet been cost-effective. The workers tend to range widely rather than staying in the vicinity of the nest, and because the colonies are very small compared to those of honeybees, many colonies are needed. If colonies are purchased commercially, this may be an expensive proposition. Still, research goes on. Of course one need not buy bumblebees; if a crop needing bee pollinators can be grown without pesticides in the vicinity of good nesting and foraging habitat, it is likely that one could draw sufficient pollinators from the local populations of wild bees. Growers are understandably reluctant to gamble on this, however, or to abandon the convenience of combining insecticide treatments with transportable hives, or "pollination units."

One crop for which bumblebees have been enthusiastically adopted by growers is the hothouse tomato. Honeybees are poor performers in green-house situations, and the anthers of tomato flowers release little pollen unless they are "buzzed," a behavior that honeybees do not perform but bumblebees do. Supplying pollination for this particular crop has depended on recent advances in the technology of rearing bumblebee colonies (see "Bumblebee Cultivation").

Although bumblebees can certainly be good for agriculture, agriculture is not usually good for bumblebees. Data from North America are sparse, but changes in the range and abundance of bumblebees have been well documented in Great Britain and some areas of Europe (P. H. Williams 1982, 1986). Before 1960, fourteen *Bombus* species occurred in east-central England; seven of these remain now. Similarly, of thirty-one species in France and Belgium, ten have declined and four have disappeared (P. H. Williams, Corbet, and Osborne. 1991). Ironically, areas of low bumblebee density often correspond to areas of intensive agriculture where bumblebees should be most valued. The number of bumblebees present in crop fields is signifi-cantly higher where untamed land remains in the form of pastures, mead-ows, and forests (P. H. Williams 1986) that provide nesting sites and forage for bees. Bumblebees prefer perennial flowers with long corolla tubes, and these types of flowers grow in areas of low disturbance (Dramstad and Fry 1995; Fussell and Corbet 1992). Weedy, shallow-tubed annuals are more abundant on disturbed land. Undisturbed hedgerow vegetation, once a promi-nent component of European farms, can therefore be significant in maintaining pollinator populations. Of particular importance are hedgerow willows and a succession of flowering perennials that provide bee forage throughout the season (Osborne, P. H. Williams, and Corbet 1991). Mechanization of agriculture has allowed cultivation of what were once considered marginal lands. European hedgerow loss began in the mid-1800s, followed by declines in wild plants and pollinators. Since 1938, Britain has lost 30 percent of its hedgerows. Certain regions of Belgium lost from 5 to 80 percent between 1960 and 1990 (Osborne, P. H. Williams, and Corbet 1991). With the reduction in floral variety, native pollinators decline, resulting in negative effects on crop pollination.

Although bee-visited crops do provide nectar or pollen, their flowering periods are usually brief. Therefore they are unable to sustain a bumblebee colony throughout the summer. Because crop production suffers when pollinators decline, some farmers switch to growing cereals or other wind-pollinated plants. These crops do not support pollinators, thus resulting in further declines of bee populations (Gauld, Collins, and Fitton 1990).

Grazing

Grazing can dramatically change the composition of range vegetation. Selective grazing by livestock can change growth forms so that few flowers are produced, and it can eliminate some species while favoring the growth of plants that livestock ignore (Gess and Gess 1993). Cattle often reduce the availability of bee food plants. For example, in riparian areas, willow shrubs serve as cattle browse, and large numbers of cattle can decimate willow cover (Sampson 1952). Willow flowers are critical resources for queen bees in the early spring when few other pollen sources are available. Livestock also trample bumblebee nests and compact the earth, often making it unsuitable for ground-nesting bee species (Sugden 1985).

Pesticides and Herbicides

Pesticides applied to crop fields or to rangelands can also exact a high mortality on bees. A dramatic demonstration of the effects of pesticides occurred in the 1970s when forests in New Brunswick, Canada, were sprayed with fenitrothion to control spruce budworm, a caterpillar that attacks forest trees. Although the spray was aimed at forests, it would occasionally drift onto adjacent blueberry fields. The biology of the budworm meant that the spray had to be applied in the spring when bumblebee queens were active, both in the fields and in the forest. The populations of bumblebees and other wild bees were devastated; fenitrothion is extremely toxic to bees. As Kevan (1974) noted, blueberry growers felt a double economic impact: first, poor pollination limited the size of their crops; second, the blueberries that did mature were eagerly sought by birds that were driven out of the forests by hunger because the wild fruit plants, such as dogwood, had also gone unpollinated. Wildflowers in the area, such as lady's slipper orchids, also suffered reduced pollination as a result of the pesticide campaign (see Kevan 1998, 1975a and b; Kevan, Clark, and Thomas 1990; Kevan and Plowright 1989; Plowright and Rodd 1980).

Rangelands are often sprayed with pesticides to control grasshoppers that consume grass that would otherwise be available to livestock. Several endangered rangeland plants require bee pollination, and their reproduction could be negatively affected as wild bees succumb to the pesticides (Bowlin, Tepedino, and Griswold 1993; Peach et al. 1993). U.S. law prohibits spraying within 3 miles of a known population of endangered plants, yet whether this arbitrary distance is sufficient to protect the plants' pollinators is hard to say—not enough is yet known about the foraging distances of many bee species.

Herbicides, applied to roadside and agricultural areas, decrease the availability of floral food for bees, ultimately decreasing bee populations (Kevan 1991). Herbicide use has been implicated in reduced pollination of blueberries, orchard fruits, and cranberries (Kevan 1991). Rather than using herbicides to maintain neat road verges, highway departments could (and occasionally do) plant low-maintenance wildflower mixes to encourage bees, butterflies, and beneficial insects.

Competition from Honeybees

Bumblebees and honeybees are both generalists, feeding on a wide variety of flowers. In *Bumblebee Economics*, Heinrich (1979) states that there is broad overlap in the diets of bumblebees and honeybees, and consequently the potential for great competition between them. Heinrich's calculations indicate that one honeybee colony can in principle prevent the production of more than thirty thousand bumblebee reproductives. The extent of this competition in the field needs further study. In Europe, where honeybees are native, some species of bumblebees have longer tongues than honeybees. These suffer less competition so long as deep-flowered perennials are present (P. H. Williams 1986).

Bumblebees and Endangered Plants

Although estimates are available for the economic value of crop pollination, it is more difficult to assign a dollar amount to the services that wild pollinators perform for noncrop plants. Some studies of rare or endangered plants, however, show bumblebees to be critical for maintenance of plant populations. One of the problems afflicting plant populations is their patchy distribution, a problem that becomes severely exaggerated as natural habitats are fragmented by human activities. Small populations of isolated plants are unattractive to pollinators and receive fewer insect visits than plants in fields of varied floral composition. An endangered plant may receive little or no pollen from outside its small patch of closely related individuals. This can result in inbreeding or low seed set because of genetic incompatibility of close relatives.

A community-based management strategy may be required to maintain both an endangered plant and its pollinators. Consider *Spiranthes diluvialis*, a rare orchid from Colorado and Utah. It requires pollinators, generally bumblebees, for sexual reproduction. Many populations of this plant grow on public rangeland subject to pesticide spraying. Government rules prohibit spraying pesticides in the area of known populations of endangered plants. These pesticide-free zones will be required to maintain viable bumblebee populations. *Spiranthes* also grows along stream banks subject to flooding. At least one pollinating bumblebee species nests below ground and could benefit from the provision of nest boxes. Although the orchid provides nectar for bumblebees, other flowering species must coexist near the *Spiranthes* populations to provide the pollen bees require. Therefore, management plans must consider the floral diversity of the community as well as the endangered plant (Sipes and Tepedino 1995).

Similarly, a European plant, *Phyteuma nigrum* (Campanulaceae), endangered in the Netherlands, requires long-tongued bumblebees for seed production. Bumblebees rarely visit small or remote populations of the plant, and are unlikely to move between localized patches unless they are surrounded by other flowers attractive to bumblebees (Kwak et al. 1991). Habitat management for floral diversity may be the most important factor in maintaining pollinator populations (K. W. Richards 1993). In Hokkaido, Japan, populations of the wild primrose "sakura-sou" (*Primula sieboldii*: Primulaceae) are restricted to small fragments of oak forest separated by agricultural pasture. The long-tubed, self-incompatible, spring-blooming flowers appear adapted for pollination by queens of the long-tongued *Bombus diversus*. In some of the forest patches, *B. diversus* has been extirpated or is extremely rare; in those patches the primrose has poor seed set. It has been shown that this is due to insufficient pollination rather than other causes, because bumblebees' claws leave white scars on the magenta petals. Seed production is correlated with claw-mark frequency (Washitani 1996).

Bumblebee Cultivation

Commercial cultivation of bumblebees began in the late 1980s in the Netherlands and Belgium (de Ruijter 1997). The groundwork for commercialization had been laid by Sladen's (1912) pioneering work, with refinements added more recently by Röseler (1985) and others. These techniques were fine-tuned to allow industrial-scale production of bumblebees for pollination of greenhouse tomatoes, a role in which honeybees had been tried with little success. First, honeybees tend to leave greenhouses if there are good resources outside. Second, even when they stay inside, they work the flowers poorly. Tomato flowers have salt shaker–like "poricidal" anthers that do not split open and spill out pollen as most flowers do, but open only a small terminal pore through which pollen grains can exit. They are best pollinated by bees that vibrate the anthers to extract the pollen (Buchmann 1983). Until bumblebees were available commercially, most greenhouse tomatoes were hand-pollinated, often with small, handheld, electric vibrators that simulated the pollen-buzzing behavior of bees. Bumblebees were seen as an alternative to this expensive, labor-intensive hand pollination.

Most bumblebee species have single annual life cycles; maximum colony size does not synchronize with commercial pollination needs. Successful commercial cultivation was dependent on the development of techniques that could alter the seasonal timing of the life cycle and availability of bees. In 1985, Röseler discovered that queens treated with carbon dioxide were tricked into forgoing their six-month hibernation; they would start laying eggs within a few weeks of treatment (Hughes 1996). This key discovery allowed year-round production of bumblebee workers. Corporate researchers have surely made a number of other technological advances, but unfortunately for amateurs and basic researchers, these are closely held trade secrets. Chapter 6 summarizes the major aspects of bombiculture that have become public knowledge.

Use of bumblebees in greenhouses is so successful that the practice has spread throughout the world, and commercial bees are available from sources in Europe, North America, and New Zealand (see Appendix 2). A side effect of the use of bumblebees in greenhouses has been the substitution of biological controls for pesticides that would harm bees. Indeed, the principal supplier of commercial bumblebees (Koppert) is also in the business of biological control; essentially, they offer growers a novel package of biological pollination and pest control. A second effect resulting from the nonseasonal availability of bumblebees has been the purchase of colonies for education and research, because they can now be studied indoors at any time.

Bumblebee Introductions

Although bumblebee declines are of great concern, in some parts of the world bumblebees are not welcome. Bumblebees have been introduced to several countries where they are not native. Four species of bumblebees were shipped to New Zealand in 1885 (Donovan 1990) to pollinate red clover, an imported forage crop. New Zealand lacks native long-tongued bees, and the introduced bumblebees were considered to be a great success because of their effectiveness at pollinating the crop. More recently, one of these introduced species, *Bombus ruderatus*, was exported from New Zealand to Chile for clover pollination (Arretz and Macfarlane 1986). *B. terrestris*, however, a relatively short-tongued species and a robber, has also been introduced to Tasmania, Israel, and Japan, where its presence is deplored by conservationists because it may compete with native species and introduce diseases harmful to the natives. Attempts to remove the bumblebees from Tasmania have met with little success.

Commercial suppliers exported European *Bombus terrestris* to Japan to pollinate greenhouse tomatoes, but the fertilized queens escaped from the greenhouses, and the aggressive queens began to take over nests of native Japanese bumblebees. One can understand that Japanese tomato growers would be eager to acquire the newest pollinating technology, but their rush to bring in foreign bees was unfortunate, probably irreversible, and almost certainly unnecessary. Nine of the fifteen bumblebees native to Japan have been raised in laboratory colonies, and several are comparable in efficiency to *B. terrestris* as tomato pollinators. Bee biologists recommend using these native species in greenhouses to avoid any additional ecological harm from *B. terrestris* (Ono, Mitsuhata, and Sasaki 1994; Asada and Ono 1996).

Public Education

Large-scale bumblebee surveys in Europe have helped document bee phenology, range, and preferred food plants. National bumblebee surveys in England were organized by the Watch Trust for Environmental Education and the London Wildlife Trust. Most of the participants were children. In the Netherlands the surveys were organized by the Royal Dutch Society for Nature Observation, the Dutch Youth Society for Nature Study, and the Dutch Natural History Society of Limburg (Matheson 1996). These surveys provided useful information and helped develop public awareness and enthusiasm for bumblebees. School programs and class field projects help students develop the skills they need to study bumblebees, and make children more mindful of the vital role that bumblebees play in the natural community. Monitoring programs for particular types of hymenopteran populations can serve as good general indicators of habitat quality or degradation (Day 1991).

6

Raising Bumblebees

These children of the sun which summer brings
As pastoral minstrels in her merry train
Pipe rustic ballads upon busy wings
And glad the cotters' quiet toils again.
The white-nosed bee that bores its little hole
In mortared walls and pipes its symphonies,
And never absent couzen, black as coal,
That Indian-like bepaints its little thighs,
With white and red bedight for holiday,
Right earlily a-morn do pipe and play
And with their legs stroke slumbers from their eyes.
And aye so fond they of their singing seem
That in their holes abed at close of day
They still keep piping in their honey dreams,
And larger ones that thrum on ruder pipe
Round the sweet-smelling closen and rich woods,
Where tawny white and red-flushed clover buds
Shine bonnily and bean fields, blossom ripe,
Shed dainty perfumes and give honey food
To these sweet poets of the summer field,
Me much delighting as I stroll along
The narrow path that hay laid meadow yields,
Catching the windings of their wandering song.
The black and yellow bumble first on wing
To buzz among the sallow's early flowers,
Hiding its nest in holes from fickle Spring
Who stints his rambles with her frequent showers;
And one that may for wiser piper pass,
In livery dress half sables and half red,
Who laps a moss ball in the meadow grass
And hoards her stores when April showers have fled;
And russet commoner who knows the face
Of every blossom that the meadow brings,
Starting the traveller to a quicker pace
By threatening round his head in many rings:
These sweeten summer in their happy glee
By giving for her honey melody.
                              —John Clare, "Wild Bees"

Why would anyone want to raise bumblebees? The simplest reason is pure curiosity: bees are interesting to watch. But there are more specific reasons as well: basic scientific study in animal behavior or pollination ecology, provision of pollination service for crops, and educational use in demonstration projects or independent research projects suitable for students (see Chapter 7).

Safety Note

Most people immediately associate "bees" with "stings," and sometimes that unfortunate association is enough to quell any curiosity they might have had about these animals. It is true that most bees, including bumblebees, can sting; anyone who takes up bumblebees as a serious hobby or scientific interest should be reconciled to a few stings each year. It is also true that "stinging bees" (including wasps) account for more fatalities in North America than do many other creatures with more fearsome reputations, such as spiders and venomous snakes. Death and serious injury, however, typically require one or both of two ingredients: very large colony sizes and allergic reactions by the victim. The relatively small, annual colonies of bumblebees seldom get large enough to do serious damage, even if they launch a concerted attack, which is very rare. The dangerous social insects are those, such as honeybees and hornets, that form large to immense colonies and that are active in defending their colonies. For example, the Africanized honeybee, which has established feral populations in the southern United States, is definitely dangerous to anyone who unwittingly disturbs a colony. Knowledgeable beekeepers, however, can and do handle these bees with little risk. Only a few pieces of equipment and information are sufficient to handle the small colonies of the far more passive bumblebees. One does not need a lion tamer's spirit.

Matters are different, however, if one is severely allergic to stings. Only a few stings, or even a single one, can send a sensitized victim into a state of anaphylactic shock, which can be fatal if not treated very quickly. Fortunately, most such people develop high levels of sensitivity only after repeated stings over a period of time. They experience increasingly severe reactions over time, so there is usually enough warning for them to take proper precautions against accidental stings, that is, stop working with stinging insects and carry epinephrine whenever they are outdoors. Although bumblebee venom is not identical to that of the honeybee, cross-reactions occur (Vetter and Visscher 1998) because some of the component allergens are the same.

A person with a known allergy to bee stings has no business keeping captive bees for study, even if they are as comparatively innocuous as bumblebees. Indeed, we do not recommend this pursuit to anyone who is not already confident, from repeated prior experience, that he or she can tolerate bee stings. Even so, we further recommend that anyone involved in bombiculture procure the proper emergency medical treatment for anaphylactic shock: an injectable dose of epinephrine. A special, very useful syringe is available in the United States under the trade name Epipen (see Appendix 2). Designed to be operated by a victim who is already experiencing difficulties, it is also good for those who might be clumsy or squeamish about conventional syringes. Its hidden needle injects the proper dose automatically when the unit is simply pressed against the thigh. Even beekeepers with demonstrated sting tolerance should have some such device handy for potentially susceptible visitors.

Harvesting Established Colonies from the Wild

If circumstances let you spend plenty of time in good bumblebee habitat, you may well be able to find nests in nature simply by noticing traffic at nest entrances. These entrances are likely to be completely inconspicuous holes in the ground or crevices under rocks, so you usually have to see a bee go in or out. This may seem difficult and unlikely—and so it is for an impatient observer. But it is not impossible: Harder (1986) found 35 nests in a Canadian field of 3.2 hectares (4.4 nests per acre), and Cumber (1953) found 19.75 nests per acre in a refuse dump in New Zealand. The gifted F. W. Sladen (1912), whose home in Kent, England, must have been very near to bumblebee heaven, reported that on a quiet, windless day in the right habitat, "we shall be rewarded within a few minutes by the sight of a humblebee either leaving or entering its nest." In particular, a heavily pollen-loaded worker hovering near the ground is worth a longer look.

If you let it be known that you are interested in bees, you may receive calls from neighbors whose houses have been colonized; bumblebees investigate all sorts of holes, not just rodent burrows, and they seem to find fiberglass insulation particularly suitable for nesting. Of course you are also likely to receive calls about honeybees, hornets, yellowjackets, and carpenter bees. Depending on your questions, interest, and curiosity level, these need not be disappointments.

Finding colonies in the wild is unlikely to be very successful until high summer, when the worker force reaches its pinnacle. Therefore you are unlikely to see the earliest stages of colony development. Also, of course, you are most likely to discover the biggest, most active colonies, which may cause you some concern if you decide to excavate the colony for transfer to an observation box. Nevertheless, except for particularly aggressive species (e.g., *B. fervidus*), making such a transfer is not particularly difficult if you first gather the right equipment. A bee veil or a mosquito head net will probably boost your confidence, although it is unlikely to be necessary unless something goes wrong. Light-colored clothing, including a long-sleeved shirt, is also a good idea. More importantly, you will need a trowel and several receptacles for bees. We recommend a good supply, say twenty, of plastic "snap-cap" vials; a pharmacy may be able to provide you with nonchildproof pill vials that would work well. You will also need a short-handled insect net and one or more large glass jars or, better yet, large Erlenmeyer flasks of 2- to 3-liter capacity.

The plan is to use the trowel to expose the entrance tunnel and follow it to the nest. A wire probe that can be pushed down the hole ahead of your excavation will help you find the tunnel in the probable event of collapse. While doing this, you must use the net, vials, and jars to capture bees, both returning foragers and colony defenders. When you finally reach the comb, you are likely to find the queen—whose capture naturally merits particular care—along with some smaller workers and recently emerged callow bees, none of which are likely to be very aggressive. Before you get to the comb, you will probably have encountered most of the real defense force. These defenders are likely to orient toward you as they reach the tunnel mouth, and they can usually be captured by placing a vial or jar directly over them before they are airborne. In a well-managed excavation, you proceed slowly enough so that these bees appear individually.

The less numerous returning foragers may fly around you and require the net. Sladen's (1912) elegantly simple method used two large-mouth jars and a piece of cardboard. He would catch a bee in one jar, invert it over the other with the cardboard in between, then slide out the cardboard, causing the bee to fall into the lower jar. Replacing the cardboard would trap the bee in the lower jar and free the upper jar to catch the next bee. Although this is probably the fastest method, there is some risk of upsetting the jar full of bees during these manipulations. Also, new bees may arrive on the scene before the top jar is empty to receive them. Beginners are likely to be more comfortable with a supply of vials. This way, each bee can be caught and capped individually, then dumped into a jar or flask during a lull. As your proficiency and confidence increase, you will use the vials less and less.

An even quicker method of handling the defenders is to grab them by the leg with bee forceps and dump them directly into a container. This more swashbuckling method requires good visibility, a deft touch, and the confidence that comes with practice. You will probably be comfortable with it only after you have gained experience in tending captive colonies using forceps.

After you have exposed the comb and removed all but the most timid of callows, you can pick it up and place it in a prepared nest box (see "Nest Boxes"). Be careful to maintain its original orientation, and prop it if necessary to keep it from tipping. If you intend to keep it in a warm place, you should at this time remove the covering insulation so that you can better observe the colony's activities. If you leave even a small amount of insulation, the bees will weave it into a dome that will frustrate your wish to see them.

During any of these manipulations, you may have the disquieting experience of having a bee evade all your snares and fly directly at you, intent on mayhem. A sweep of your conveniently placed net will usually snag it, but if your net is not so conveniently placed, you can usually knock the bee out of the air with a sharp, flat-handed, downward slap. A smartly slapped bee will usually lie stunned on the ground for a second or two, giving you a precious instant to pounce on it with one of your conveniently placed vials. Should a vial not come to hand, you can keep slapping while you reassess the merits of conveniently placed equipment. Such treatment does not harm the bees and it can provide high comedy to onlookers.

Bees definitely can be harmed during an excavation, however, if you leave their jar in the sun. Already overheated by their exertions, they can quickly perish if the jar is not shaded. A radical cure for this problem is to excavate at night. There are two additional advantages: the entire worker force should be home, and if you work with a red filter on a battery-powered headlamp, the bees will typically not fly at all. The principal disadvantage is that your visibility is seldom good, and it is easier to lose track of the tunnel and botch the job. On balance, daytime digs are easier unless you are particularly fearful of flying bees. To be sure of capturing the workers that are out foraging, you should expect to spend at least an hour or so at the nest. You certainly do not need to secure the entire colony to have a viable observation nest, but the spectacle of returned workers, searching for days for their stolen home, can rend the heart of anyone who has begun to appreciate bees.

INdUciNG NesTiNG by CApTiVE QUEENS

The following instructions derive mostly from lore picked up by James Thomson while in the lab of R. Chris Plowright, plus a few of his own observations. Another very useful summary of current practice is given in a series of articles by Delaplane (1995a and b, 1996 a and b). Although it is not the simplest way to obtain a colony, catching queens in spring is the most engaging and potentially most gratifying way to proceed. After suffering through the suspense of waiting for your bees to become broody, you may be lucky enough to see the entire cycle of colony development. If you succeed, you will probably cherish these animals for the rest of your life. Another advantage for the novice bee wrangler is that you will gradually start learning how to handle a box full of bees. As in making duck soup, you might expect the initial step to be "First catch a bee," but there are several indispensable preliminaries.

The most important is locating a supply of pollen. Although truly dedicated bombiculturists might be willing to spend a few hours each day manually scraping pollen out of flowers, the only really practical course is to use pollen collected by honeybees. Honey beekeepers frequently carry out "pollen trapping" by forcing returning workers to squeeze through the carefully sized meshes of a series of screens that pluck off a fraction of the corbicular loads. The pollen falls into a tray for later collection. To obtain top-grade pollen, you need to contract with a beekeeper who not only traps pollen but who also empties the traps frequently and freezes the pellets rather than simply drying them. Bumblebee queens are regally fastidious about the freshness of their pollen; although you can purchase dried "bee pollen" at health-food stores, it is expensive and not likely to please the tastes of your prospective foundress. If at all possible, use only fresh-frozen pollen and keep it frozen until use. Appendix 2 lists some reliable mail-order suppliers, but the best way to start your search is to contact a local association of beekeepers.

Bee Foods

With a few bizarre exceptions, such as some carrion-eating stingless bees of the Tropics, all bees subsist on floral nectar and pollen only. Nectar is easier to obtain than pollen because commercial honey is essentially concentrated nectar with a few other substances contributed by honeybees. It is quite suitable for feeding bumblebees after dilution with an equal volume of water. Although natural nectar contains numerous trace substances including amino acids, its principal role in bumblebee nutrition is as a source of carbohydrate for energy. It can therefore be replaced by a solution of table sugar, which is far cheaper than honey. For starting queens, however, it is useful to use honey solution or at least to add some honey to the table-sugar solution. Pure sugar has hardly any odor, and bees will discover feeders more quickly if they bear some floral scent.

Pollen can be introduced to bees in two forms. The first of these, "bee bread," is made by moistening pollen pellets with a little honey solution, then mixing or grinding until a stiff dough is formed. A mortar and pestle are ideal grinding tools, although a spoon and a small bowl will also work. Queens are started with lumps of bee bread; it can also be prepared in larger quantities for feeding to workers in captive hives. A simpler method of feeding established captive colonies, however, is to let the bees forage for dry pollen. Just spread some pellets out to dry, then powder them and present the grains in a small dish (see "Nest Boxes"). Although pollen is never presented in this way in flowers, workers still recognize the material and indulge in novel ways of collecting it, such as turning on their backs and wallowing in the dish!

NEST BOXES

You will also need nest boxes (Photograph 6-1). For a starting box, the only absolute requirements are that the box keep the queen inside, be porous or well ventilated, have some sort of honey feeder, and allow you easy access to the contents after removing the bee. These requirements are probably most easily met by an open-top plywood box with a loose glass or plastic cover that can be slid off. Cleaning—which is essential—is easier if the bottom is also loose or easily detachable. A hole bored at an angle in the side can hold a plastic syringe sans needle, which makes an inexpensive, easily cleaned gravity feeder. Starter boxes can be small (3 inches on a side) if you will later be transferring started colonies into larger quarters. It is more convenient to start queens directly in a two-compartment observation box large enough to accommodate a fully developed colony, but some species seem more likely to start in a smaller box. (Even if you plan to buy or find bees rather than rear them, we strongly recommend housing them in an observation box.)

Design is more critical in an observation box than in a starter box, because it must be capable of handling dozens of bees and their accumulating wastes as well as permit your observations and manipulations. Doing remodel carpentry on a box full of bees is to be avoided.

Warmth and Humidity

Although a well-developed colony with ad libitum food is capable of maintaining the necessary warm temperature for optimal larval development, a single queen needs help. In the wild, insulating nest materials provide this help, and the pioneers of bombiculture generally supplied nest boxes with either natural or artificial insulation. If used, insulation should be fibrous so that the bees can sculpt it into caves and canopies. Upholsterer's cotton batting works well, and an old piece of junk furniture can yield a lifetime supply. Polyester fiberfill batting also seems acceptable to bees and is cleaner to work with, but is expensive if bought new. Fiberglass insulation satisfies bees but is disagreeable for humans to handle. Styrofoam or other rigid foams can help retain warmth but cannot be sculpted and will eventually be chewed to messy bits. Because wild queens often choose mouse nests

Photograph 6-1: A plywood nest box with a Plexiglas lid permits observation of colony activities. The box is divided into two compartments. The entrance hole opens into the compartment on the right, which serves as a feeding and defecating area. The back compartment to the left contains the brood.

(Chapter 2), some culturists have allowed mice to "work over" nesting material before placing it in bee boxes. Although the idea is appealing, the practice is less so, and there seems to be no hard evidence in its favor.

Insulation has one important drawback: it makes observation much harder. A brooding queen will excavate a spherical chamber, hiding all her activities and constructions. Later on, workers will construct a domelike roof over the whole nest, reinforcing the fibers with wax. Working with such colonies requires repeatedly tearing down this cover, an operation that invites the escape of agitated workers. Therefore it is best to remove nesting material as the colony becomes thermally independent. The modern method is to eliminate insulation completely by starting queens at a high temperature. Queens of most species seem to benefit from any increase above room temperature up to about 30°C. Although few casual bee-raisers own incubators, improved rearing success can be achieved by some very simple measures, such as placing the boxes on top of a refrigerator so that they are bathed in the warm convective airflow from the rear coils. Generally speaking, spots that cause bread dough to rise strongly are good for rearing bumblebees. A more luxurious arrangement would be a closet with a small thermostatically controlled space heater. It is also desirable to keep the humidity high, which can be done simply by misting the boxes after daily inspection. If mold appears in the boxes, the humidity should be reduced, of course.

Sanitation and Ventilation

By convention, the "back" compartment of a two-room nest box is where nesting is induced. The "front" compartment houses the nectar feeder, so these compartments serve respectively as "home" and "outside" to captive bees. Bees will defecate "outside," and because bee feces are watery and copious, the front box should be designed to handle a large volume of mess over the lifetime of the colony. One simple approach is to cover the floor with a 1- to 2-cm layer of cat-box litter. Use a plain clay product in place of fancy deodorizing or clumping types. More elaborate is a floor of perforated aluminum sheet, a window screen, or 1/8-inch mesh hardware cloth, all of which allow wastes to drain through to a cleanable surface below.

If the litter method is used, screened holes should be provided in the upper sides of the front box to permit airflow. Similar holes in the rear box can be kept corked to retain warmth during early colony growth, then opened when the worker force burgeons. Use aluminum window screen; fiberglass does not withstand bees' mandibles.

Construction Materials and Techniques

Good bumblebee homes are well within the capacity of an amateur builder with home shop tools. Observation boxes for indoor use (as opposed to field domiciles) can be made of unpainted 1/2-inch plywood. (We abandon the metric system here, because North American readers will find building materials available in nominal English sizes only.) The plywood should be rated for "exterior use," which means that it is made with waterproof glue, and can be "C-D" grade, which means that there are some surface knots and voids but that most of the sheet is usable. Using thicker 3/4-inch plywood for the front wall makes it easier to drill an angled hole for the feeder. Compartment covers are best made from acrylic sheet (e.g., Plexiglas), either 1/4 or 1/8 inch thick. Hatch covers are most elegantly made from heavy, 1/2-inch acrylic, although thinner stock can be used if weighted down. Both wood and plastic parts are best cut on a table saw using a good, carbide-tipped blade with at least thirty teeth to produce square cuts with smooth surfaces that will make good butt joints. A band saw can produce acceptable results also, although you will first have to reduce large plywood sheets to more manageable proportions.

Ventilation and exit holes should be about ³/₄ inch unless another size is required by your choice of tunnel materials. Feeder holes, if used, should fit the size of syringe. Although they can be bored with inexpensive spade bits in a handheld electric drill, these will be splintery and rough. A more expensive Forstner bit—best used in a drill press—does a much better job, especially for the angled feeder holes. The large hatches in the front and back acrylic covers are essential for accessing the interior without allowing escapes. They are best drilled with a 2¹/₂- or 3-inch hole saw, which is a drill-driven cylinder with sawteeth. Hole saws are best used in a drill press, but can be used in a handheld drill if you are careful to clamp the acrylic sheet to a rigid backer board of scrap material.

Boxes can be assembled with nails, but they will last longer if glued and screwed. Hot-melt glue, although handy for making temporary assemblies, lacks strength and permanence. Even white or yellow carpenter's glue will not stand up to weather or to the repeated washing that bee equipment requires, so use a waterproof glue (e.g., two-component resorcinol glue (Weldwood) or the newer waterproof yellow glues (Elmer's, Titebond) or the even newer polyurethane types (Excel). By far the best screws are squarehead or Robertson screws. For ¹/₂-inch plywood construction, use 1 inch by number 6 flathead Robertson screws. If you drive them with a cordless power screwdriver, you need not drill pilot holes first. A thread lubricant (beeswax, naturally!) eases insertion. Check the box for squareness and alignment at each step of assembly.

Construction Options for Food Supply, Access, and Traffic Control. The queen must be kept captive, of course. Workers, however, can be confined in the box or allowed to forage freely. If you plan to confine the workers, you must be able to introduce large amounts of sugar-water and pollen. For an inexpensive, large-volume nectar feeder, you can use a gravity water dispenser made for birdcages. This has an open dispensing trough that protrudes from the bottom like a small foot. For use with bees, this trough should be filled with a piece of cellulose sponge, from which the bees can collect solution when it is saturated. Should you use this method, you must make some arrangement for replacing the large feeder without allowing escapes. Probably the best method is to mount the feeder outside the box, and insert the trough in a hole in the side wall.

For feeding pollen to a large colony, the simplest method is to use dry pollen, as described. If you locate the pollen dish under a ¹/₂-inch hole drilled in the plastic cover of the front box, the dry pollen can be dumped in through this hole without letting the bees escape. Be sure to mount the dish and any nectar feeders above the floor of the box to avoid contamination from feces. By these means a colony can be kept going in the lab even in winter.

In good weather, however, it is usually more rewarding to let the colony feed itself by allowing the workers to forage outdoors. The box can simply be placed outdoors in a protected location, or it may be kept indoors and equipped with a tunnel to the outside. Bees will eventually discover and use tunnels of several meters in length, although shorter ones are preferable. Almost any sort of pipe will serve. Clear plastic tubing is good because the bees can be seen coming and going, and it is easy to add traffic gates by sawing nearly through the tube and dropping in a piece of card as needed. However, any impermeable tubing can become fouled by feces. An inexpensive tunnel of aluminum window screening has the triple advantages of visibility, drainage, and flexibility. To make one, cut window screen material about 6 inches wide, wrap a suitable length around a broomstick to make a tube, and secure the tube with a spiral wrapping of string. The ends of the tube can be secured to nest boxes by cutting flaps and thumbtacking them down, or by hot-melt glue. If such a tube is to be removed and replaced frequently, its ends can be fitted with short lengths of plastic pipe (e.g., $^{1}/_{2}$-inch [nominal dimension] PVC drainpipe), and the nest box exit hole can be fitted with matching PVC fittings. To induce bees to investigate and use a new tunnel of this sort, you can dribble droplets of honey-water along the screen.

Especially in the early stages of colony development, the queen may wish to continue foraging; this poses an unacceptable risk of her being lost. It is prudent to make a "queen includer" plate out of a piece of sheet metal (a soda can will suffice, but cardboard will not). Cut a rectangular opening large enough for workers to squeeze through with a little effort, but too small for the queen. Attach this to the nest box at the tunnel entrance. The correct size depends on the species and the individual queen, but it is probably smaller than you would expect.

For certain observations you may wish to intercept workers as they arrive home or depart. This can be done by replacing a section of tunnel with a removable bee vial with a hole cut (or melted) in the bottom to allow through traffic. When a bee approaches, this vial can be replaced with a standard one to catch the bee. A deluxe version of this arrangement (see Photograph 6-2) includes a section of tunnel that can detain bees briefly in the manner of a "squeeze chute" used for cattle (see "Bee Wrangling").

Rearing Bees

Now you are ready to catch your queens. Wetlands with abundant willows make good hunting sites for the earliest species, but if your environment is more suburban, you can do well at less "natural" flower sources such as dandelion-choked lawns and ornamental shrubs. A nursery with many species of flowering plants is an excellent place to find a progression of bee

Photograph 6-2: The squeeze chute can be connected by tubing to the nest box in order to catch workers as they enter the nest. The foam block is used to pin a bee to the mesh section. The deluxe model in the photograph includes a small, bottomless plastic vial that normally forms part of the tube system. The bees become used to passing through the plastic vial to enter the nest. If a bee must be captured, the plastic vial can be replaced by a closed vial to trap the bee.

species throughout the spring. You can use an insect net to catch bees, but, as described under "Bee Wrangling," they can frequently be snagged with a vial alone. If you collect at a nursery, this method will placate the proprietor. Keep the captured bees cool and dark until you get them home; a small cooler with an ice pack is ideal. Because you want bees fresh out of hibernation that have not started their own nests yet, concentrate on collecting individuals with unfaded colors and unworn wings. Do not collect bees with pollen loads in their corbiculae, as these are already committed to a nest in the wild.

In the first days, when the queen is the only inhabitant of the starter box, the best way for you to work in one box is to wait until she is in the other box. Then cut off her access with a piece of card or by sliding the smaller box so that the matching holes no longer align. This is less distressing than picking her up, and you want to avoid disturbance as much as possible.

Prepare a pea-sized lump of fresh bee bread by adding drops of diluted honey to some pollen pellets (see "Bee Foods"). If you are using insulation, make a rough cave in the insulation and adhere the lump to the bottom center with a drop of honey. If you are trying the no-insulation technique, provide some sort of cup or container, such as a plastic bottle cap, to hold the starting lump. Along with providing a nectar-syrup feeder, this is all you need do. Cover the box to exclude light—some species are insensitive to light, but others seem to prefer darkness—and resist the temptation to bother the queen for twenty-four hours. If things go well and the queen quickly becomes broody, you will start seeing the following encouraging events.

The bee will refine your rough cave into a smoothly lined, spherical cavity. She will start eating the pollen, which you can verify by noting mandible marks on the pollen lump and by noting yellow, pollen-laden feces in the front box. (Provide her with a smooth pollen lump, so that you can easily tell if she has roughened the surface.) She may daub the interior of the cavity with droplets of nectar, and she will start building a delicate honeypot of yellowish wax, usually between the pollen lump and the entrance. She will fill this pot with syrup from the feeder. The nectar you provide will allow her to feed without interrupting her incubation. Eventually she will establish a brood cell on the lump. This begins with low walls of wax. She will lay some eggs within the walls, then cover the cell with more wax. Of course you do not want to disturb the nest at this time, but you should add fresh slivers of pollen dough around the developing nest clump every day or two. You must pay attention to the quantity and fate of these slivers if you are to avoid overfeeding or underfeeding. Start with a daily pollen volume equal to about 25 percent of that of the brood clump. If pollen remains unconsumed, remove the old pieces with forceps, and cut back on the amount of fresh dough that you provide to replenish the nest. If the pollen disappears completely, increase the ration. If you see larvae that have been evicted from their cells, the nest is definitely pollen-starved.

Few queens will start nesting immediately after capture, and the majority will not start at all. If, instead of forming a cavity, your bee ignores the nesting chamber or tunnels aimlessly through the cotton, she is not yet ready to nest. So long as she has not started constructing a cell on the pollen lump, you should replace the lump with a fresh one daily. You must also check your syrup feeder to make sure that it has not begun to ferment. Cloudiness is a bad sign. Replacing the feeder daily is good hygiene. You should give a queen at least ten days to develop broodiness before giving up on her, although if she is obviously unhealthy, you may do better to release her sooner.

A recent discovery is that some queens will start faster and more reliably if they are given a worker force comprising a few callow workers of either bumblebees or (surprisingly) honeybees (van Heemert, de Ruijter, and van den Eijnde 1990). This is worth trying if you have access to honeybee hives.

After the successful emergence of the first brood, you can carefully transfer the bees and the entire brood clump to a larger observation box. You may continue to provide all of their food or make arrangements for them to forage outdoors. The latter option is better for several reasons: nest hygiene is much improved, overfeeding or underfeeding is less likely, you are spared the difficult task of introducing fresh feeders without having bees escape, and you have the opportunity to observe the foragers as they leave and return, surely one of the most interesting aspects of the whole process. Remember, however, that if you see ejected larvae in the nest, you should feed supplemental pollen; if the honeypots are dry and empty, you should squirt in some sugar syrup.

Probabilities of Success

Different bumblebee species vary widely in their adaptability to nesting in confinement. Of North American bees, the most ready starters include, unsurprisingly, the species that have been adopted by commercial suppliers: *Bombus impatiens* in the East and *B. terricola occidentalis* (usually called by the older name *B. occidentalis* in the world of commercial bumblebees) in the west. Fortunately, both have wide ranges and are easy to identify (see color plates). *B. huntii*, *B. perplexus* (R. Owen, personal communication), *B. terricola terricola*, and *B. affinis* are also amenable species. New amateurs should concentrate on these if possible. Delaplane (1995b) claims that 30 percent of *B. impatiens* can be started. Owen (personal communication) reports 80 percent success rates with *B. perplexus* and also indicates that the critical condition for success is using only very fresh new queens, in which case you can expect success rates of 50 percent or higher for most species. Other bees in the subgenera *Pyrobombus* and *Bombus* are worth trying, although some *Pyrobombus*, such as *ternarius*, are difficult. The subgenus *Fervidobombus* seems particularly resistant to this sort of domestication, which is probably just as well, given the aggressiveness of this group.

Setting Out Nest Boxes

A hands-off way to obtain study colonies is to set out nest boxes in suitable habitats where numerous queens are searching for nests. Many designs have been tried for such domiciles, but the "standard" is a simple box of ³/₄-inch exterior-grade plywood, about 8 by 8 by 6 inches, with an appropriately sized (about ⁵/₈-inch) hole in one side and an overhanging roof that is hinged for easy observation. Such boxes should be painted for longevity, but avoid oil-based paints and paint them well before setting them out in the early spring. You must supply insulation. By far the best site is a south-facing bank. Some bee species may prefer underground boxes fitted with entrance tunnels of plastic pipe. You may be able to fool some of these subterranean species by equipping an aboveground box with a longer tunnel that dips underground, then resurfaces. Provide drainage holes so that the low spots of the tunnel do not fill with rainwater.

Before reusing outdoor domiciles, add fresh insulation each season and clean the boxes thoroughly to discourage parasites. For this reason, one published domicile design specifies the use of easily scrubbed "plastic lumber," but this material may be difficult to find. In our experience, outdoor domiciles can have high occupancy rates, but many colonies fail because of ants, excess moisture during bad weather, and sometimes attack by the mammalian predators noted previously.

Buying Bumblebee Colonies

Until the 1990s anyone wanting a bumblebee colony for study needed to find a wild colony or start one following the techniques we have outlined. Things have changed! The recent development of bumblebees for commercial pollination of tomatoes and other greenhouse crops makes it possible to purchase colonies year-round from agricultural suppliers, at least in Europe, North America, Japan, and New Zealand (see Appendix 2). This is likely to be the best method for classroom use, as most school calendars seem to have been devised with scandalous disregard of the life cycles of local bumblebees.

Although colony prices were initially exorbitant in the early days of commercialization, technological advances and increasing supply have brought prices down. At this writing, Koppert supplies small colonies for $200, with substantial discounts if the bees are for research. Large colonies, which cost more, are better for pollinating large acreages of crops under glass, but provide no advantage for research and education.

Indeed, it is much better to receive a small colony, in the early stages of colony growth, than a big one, because you will usually want to transfer the colony from its shipping container to a more suitable box for viewing and manipulating the bees. Colonies from Koppert, for example, come with a cottonlike insulation that the bees typically work into an opaque, waxy dome over the entire comb. This renders invisible all activity except out-of-hive foraging. Furthermore, because this pollination system is optimized for pollination of tomatoes by pollen collectors, the colony boxes contain a very large concealed reservoir of sugar syrup. If you plan to conduct experiments involving nectar foraging, you need to remove this cornucopia before the bees will cooperate. Transferring a large colony from its shipping container to an observation box is quite straightforward, but it is definitely an occasion for full protective clothing, including gloves and a head net.

Although commercial suppliers sometimes ship exotic bees, we urge readers to purchase only species that are native to the area. Even if you are using a correct species, if it comes from a different region, escapees from your purchased colony might still introduce new genes or diseases to your area. Therefore, such colonies are best restricted to indoor use. Recall that, although workers are considered "sterile," they can in fact lay fertile male eggs. Starting your own colonies of local species is definitely the most responsible technique.

Bee Wrangling

Handling bumblebees can be eased by several sorts of devices. Whenever you work with a colony, keep a short-handled insect net handy. Plastic snap-cap vials are very useful. They can be used without modification if bees are housed in them for only a few minutes, but it is better to punch several holes in the polyethylene caps to allow airflow. An inexpensive leather punch will do a particularly neat job, but is hardly necessary. Keep the holes small, no larger than $1/8$ inch, because you may need to retain some dwarfed workers, who can definitely squeeze through a $1/4$-inch hole. It is also good to wad some tissue or toilet paper into the bottom of the vial to help absorb water. A bit of sponge works as well.

The classic method of getting a bee into a vial is to catch it in an insect net, then introduce the opened vial into the net so as to work the bee into the vial. As the bee enters the vial, push the open end of the vial against the net fabric so that the fabric stretches across the opening like the head of a drum. Watch to see when the bee lets go of the fabric and falls down into the vial, then slide the vial cap on from the side, slipping it between the stretched fabric and the opening of the vial. Hold the cap on loosely while you check the position of the bee. Do not snap on the cap until you are sure that the bee does not have a leg on the rim of the vial.

In many situations, bumblebees can be popped into vials directly, without first being netted. This is particularly true when they are in a flight cage or on the comb, but they can also be taken while feeding on many sorts of flowers. The best flowers for such direct captures are large tubular ones—like foxgloves or penstemons—that completely contain the bees. If you position the vial over a flower while the bee is feeding, she will usually back out right into the vial.

Although vials have their uses, it is often quicker to grasp bees directly with forceps. This takes a little more skill and practice. Do not try to grip the body; grab for the legs. With six possibilities, it is surprisingly easy to get a good grip on a leg. Although bee legs seem very fragile things for gripping with steel forceps, they are actually quite tough. If you use good forceps without too much spring to them, it is very unlikely you will hurt the bee. Although they are expensive, the best forceps are those made for eye surgery. They have a very gentle action plus doubly serrated tips that grip without slipping.

Marking bees requires holding them still. We call our favorite apparatus a "bee squeezer" (Photograph 6-3). The essential elements are a tube with one end open and the other end covered with a coarse fabric mesh, plus a foam-topped plunger that fits inside the tube. By getting the bee into the tube, then pushing in the plunger, the bee can be immobilized between the foam and the mesh. Any device that accomplishes this immobilization will be useful, and large syringes have been used. The design in Photograph 6-3 has some subtle refinements, however. The tube portion is a polypropylene vial with an integral hinged cap. The bottom inch or so is sawed off. The snap cap is not removed, but the center of the cap is, leaving just a ring. This can be done with a sharp knife, but the polypropylene is tough to cut. An easier way, if you have the tool, is to sand down the cap with a coarse belt sander until only the outer rim remains. With the center removed, a piece of the mesh can be stretched across the opening, then retained in place by snapping down the rim. The plunger is a plain polystyrene bee vial with a 1-inch thick piece of polyurethane foam fastened to the closed end with silicone adhesive. Both the foam and the mesh, which should have hexagonal openings about $1/8$ inch across, are available at fabric stores. Glue an oversized piece of foam to the polystyrene vial with silicone cement, then trim it with a razor knife until it can enter the larger tube smoothly.

An advantage of this design over a syringe is that the whole assembly can stand flat on a tabletop. More subtly, if the outer tube is sawed off at the right height, it will grasp the slightly tapered plunger vial by friction just as the plunger is pushed home. Thus the clamping pressure on the bee is maintained without the necessity of holding the two pieces together manually. This leaves both your hands free to attend to your prisoner. Spare pieces of foam and mesh are conveniently stored in the plunger vial.

A bee is most easily marked after you have maneuvered it so that the dorsal thorax is pressed through a hole in the mesh. Frequently a bee will obligingly move into this position as you alternately withdraw and press in the plunger. Some recalcitrant bees, however, tend to hang upside down from the mesh. To turn a bee right-side-up, back out the plunger until the bee is near the edge of the tube. Trap it in this position, then roll the bee over by rotating the plunger inside the outer tube.

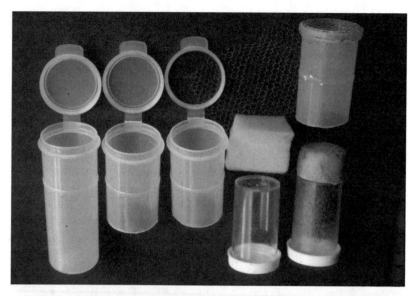

Photographs 6-3 (a) and (b): The bee squeezer is a simple device that immobilizes the bee while the investigator examines it. It is useful when making species identifications, removing pollen loads, or tagging bees with identifying marks. (a): Stages of construction of the bee squeezer. (b): A worker bee immobilized for marking within the bee squeezer.

Marks are best applied to the dorsal thorax between the wing bases (the interalar area). An easy way to mark bees is with fine, felt-tipped paint pens such as the DecoColor line made by Marvy (Uchida of America Corp., Carson, CA). Kwak (in Matheson 1996) describes a clever marking scheme whereby four dots of only five colors can allow many individuals to be marked distinctively. Be aware that similar colors such as red and orange may be hard to distinguish in the field. Apply a minimum of paint, and try to keep it away from the wing bases. If you put on too much paint, work quickly to release the bee before the paint hardens. If the bee can start moving its wings right away, it should be fine. If the bee can't fly after its release, recapture it in the bee squeezer and use fine forceps to remove paint from the wing bases.

The specified mesh is large enough to allow not only paint marking but also glue-on labels. Commercial plastic labels (Opalith-plättchen; see Appendix 2) made in Germany are available from beekeeping suppliers. A set includes the numerals 1 to 99 in each of five colors. These labels are dish-shaped, which helps them conform to the interalar area where they should be glued. The adhesive sold with the labels is, in our opinion, inferior to gel-type cyanoacrylate "super glue" cement, which sets faster. (Make sure you have the gel sort of cement, as the more liquid types are too difficult to apply without injuring the bees.) Squeeze a scant drop of cement onto a nonporous surface, use fine forceps to touch the label to the drop, and apply the label through a hole in the mesh, being careful not to sandwich a thread between the label and the bee. Homemade color labels can be cut from colored or painted acetate sheet. For adding numbers, one could use various photographic methods to produce symbols on film. Alternatively, a laser printer could make small symbols on plastic sheets designed for overhead projection. We have used photographic film, first painted white, then adorned with color-coding paint stripes, then sealed with polyurethane varnish. (Without the varnish, the paint is too quickly scraped away.) Because bees can get their claws under the edge, these flat labels are more easily dislodged than the dished commercial product, but a well-glued label will probably last for the life of a worker.

The choice of a marking technique depends on several factors. If one is marking foraging workers in the field, the fastest way is to net a bee, immobilize her by pinching her into a fold of the net, and apply liquid paint directly through the mesh of the net. This is likely to produce sloppy marks, however, and will probably kill some bees through inadvertent painting of the wing bases. The best marks for long-term study are glued-on labels. For lab studies, numbered labels are fine, but for field observations, colors may be easier to distinguish from a distance.

7

Research Projects

Some things that fly there be—
Birds—Hours—the Bumblebee—
Of these no Elegy.

Some things that stay there be—
Grief—Hills—Eternity—
Nor this behooveth me.

There are that resting, rise.
Can I expound the skies?
How still the Riddle lies!

—Emily Dickinson

Investigating Decision-Making Behavior with "Interview Bouquets"

James Thomson has used "interview bouquets" with free-foraging bees both for research questions (e.g., Thomson 1981; Thomson, Maddison, and Plowright 1982) and for exercises in university-level classes in behavioral ecology. It can be employed with any sufficiently abundant pollinator, not just bumblebees, and is quite safe. Even younger students can engage in this experiment. The lab handout reproduced on the following pages gives most of the necessary information. (Readers may reproduce the handout pages.) It requires a stand of flowering plants that is heavily visited; in the northeastern United States, these conditions can usually be met in September in old fields with goldenrods or other "weeds." Basically, one places two flowers or inflorescences (that differ in some way) at the end of a stick. By proffering the stick to a free-foraging bee and seeing which of the two options the bee chooses, one can "interview" a large number of animals about their foraging preferences. The resulting data are perfectly suited to introducing chi-squared tests of frequency data.

A crude interview stick can be cobbled together from a shrub branch and some duct tape, but a better one can be quickly made as follows (Photograph 7-1, page 112). Drill a $1/16$-inch hole about $3/8$ inch from the end of a 24-inch dowel rod or bamboo plant stake of $\frac{1}{4}$- to $\frac{3}{8}$-inch diameter. Insert a 6- to 7-inch piece of malleable wire (e.g., baling wire) through the hole, center the wire, wrap each end two turns around the rod, and twist the ends together with pliers so the wire tightly grabs the rod with the two free ends sticking out like whiskers. Take a 2-inch-long piece of clear plastic tubing (e.g., Tygon) with an internal diameter of $\frac{3}{16}$ to $\frac{1}{4}$ inch and fill about $\frac{1}{2}$ inch of one end with hot-melt glue from an electric gun. Push the glued end over one "whisker," let the glue set, then repeat for the second whisker. If you wish, you can fill the tubes with water to keep the flowers fresher, but for most purposes this will not be necessary. If the cut flower stems do not stay in place through friction alone, bend over the bottom half inch of stem to grip the tube's walls, or wedge them in place with a bit of plant material. Bend the wires so that you can present the two stimuli side by side at realistic angles.

The next few pages are taken from a laboratory handout used at SUNY-Stony Brook. Classes of about twenty students are able to complete this exercise in one afternoon, gathering enough data to make most of the indicated tests statistically significant. We hope that readers will see that many other variations are possible. For example, students capable of independent work could do significant publishable work on floral constancy, guided by the paper by Chittka, Thomson, and Waser (1999).

Behavioral Ecology Lab: Decision-Making by Foraging Bees

Animals seeking food in natural environments face a tremendous number of choices. Natural selection is expected to favor efficient foraging patterns; this expectation forms the basis of a large body of *optimal foraging theory* and associated tests. Bees have been widely used in such studies. We will investigate several types of choices that bees encounter frequently while feeding at flowers, and try to establish the *decision rules* the bees have developed to deal with these choices in nature.

Procedure

We will be presenting free-foraging bees with choice tests in the field, in a situation analogous to the T-maze (or Y-maze) design used in many lab experiments in behavioral psychology. We use a stick with two short pieces of plastic tubing at the end to hold two different flowers or inflorescences. By extending the stick toward a forager in such a way that the two flowers are equidistant from the animal, and observing which one the animal chooses to visit, one can gradually build up a large sample of decisions.

We can easily record two sorts of data. Most simply we can just record the number of times that bees make each of the two choices. We can analyze those data by a chi-squared goodness-of-fit test, against the null hypothesis that we expect equal numbers of visits to the two flowers. A significant test result indicates a feeding preference. We can also record data on the behavior of the bee after it lands on an inflorescence. These data could include things like the time spent or the number of florets probed. We will collect data (separately) for two taxa of bees, honeybees (*Apis mellifera*) and bumblebees (*Bombus* spp.). We may encounter several species of *Bombus*, but we will not try to distinguish them. We'll demonstrate how to recognize the bees, carry out the interviews, and record the data.

We will consider four general questions:

1. *Flower constancy.* In many situations bees become "constant" on a particular flower species, meaning, they visit it to the exclusion of other species they encounter. This has obvious implications for the successful cross-pollination of plants. Constancy is seldom absolute, especially when two plants are very similar; also, different types of bees are thought to differ in their levels of constancy. We will determine whether bumble bees and honeybees show constancy to goldenrod species.

   Design. Find bees feeding on one goldenrod (*Solidago*) species (say, *S. rugosa*) in an area where another species (e.g., *S. graminifolia*) is nearby or intermingled. Give these bees a choice between inflorescences of *S. rugosa* (constant) and *S. graminifolia* (inconstant). Try to make the inflorescences the same size. Ideally, do the reverse experiment with the same inflorescences (e.g., test bees coming from *S. graminifolia* also). (Why?) Record data separately for honeybees and bumblebees.

2. *Floral advertising.* The showy parts of flowers (usually petals) are thought to function primarily in pollinator attraction. In some composite heads there seems to have been an evolved division of labor between the central disk florets and the peripheral ray florets. Although in some cases the ray florets retain sexual function, in other cases they are either male-sterile or completely sterile. They also often have large, brightly colored, petal-like extensions. We will test the hypothesis that the ray florets of *Centaurea maculosa* play a role in attraction.

   Design. Cut two heads of *Centaurea maculosa*, taking them from the same plant and matching them as nearly as possible for age and size (i.e., number of florets). With your fingers, remove the ray florets from one head only; leave the other intact. How can you control for the possibility that the bees might react to scents from your fingers? Again, record data separately for the two types of bee.

3. *Nectar rewards.* Many animal-pollinated flowers produce nectar as a reward, and pollinators are known to modify their foraging behaviors in several ways in response to variations in the nectar they find (or don't find) in flowers they investigate. We are interested in several questions here: (a) Can bees detect the difference between nectar-rich and nectar-poor heads of *Centaurea maculosa* remotely, namely, without visiting and probing the flowers? (b) Do bees behave differently on rich vs. poor heads? Specifically, do they probe different numbers of flowers? (c) Do bees that have just encountered rich heads modify their subsequent foraging moves relative to those that have just visited poor heads?

   Design. We will have screened a number of flower heads to prevent visitation for twenty-four hours prior to the experiment. Pair one of these heads with a head of similar size and age that you have just seen a bee visit. Record not only which head receives the first visit by a bee, but also the number of probes the bee makes with its tongue. This will require close observation; you should be able to see a bobbing motion as if the bee were doing push-ups. Also record whether or not the bee then moves over to visit the second head of the pair, and if it does, record the number of probes there as well.

4. *Pheromone attraction.* BeeScent is a commercial product designed to attract honeybees to crop plants that need pollination. It is presumably an artificially synthesized version of mandibular gland pheromone. Does it work? If it works on honeybees, does it also work on bumblebees?

   Design. Work with a small group of classmates. What can you come up with?

Analysis

Because our design offers a pairwise choice, most of our data (Experiments 2, 3a, and 4) should be tested against the null hypothesis that bees pick each of the alternatives the same number of times, which means that, the *expected value* for the number of choices to either inflorescence would be the total number of observed choices, divided by two. If our observed results match this null expectation exactly, we know that the bees showed no preference. A perfect match is very unlikely, however. Assuming that we do not see a perfect match of observed and expected values, how do we judge whether the deviation is due to a real preference or to mere chance? Consider: if each bee were mentally flipping a coin to decide which inflorescence to visit, there would be no real preference, but simply by chance there might be an excess of "heads" or of "tails." We need a statistical test to tell us how likely it is that we could have obtained our observed results *if the null hypothesis of "no preference" were true.* If the likelihood of this is very small, we can reject that null hypothesis and conclude that the bees are really making nonrandom choices.

Because our data are frequencies, or counts of the number of times we observe a particular outcome in a series of independent trials, we can use the chi-squared test statistic to perform a *goodness-of-fit* test on the data from each set of pairwise trials.

The full analysis of constancy (Experiment 1) is slightly more complicated than a pairwise choice test, because we must consider not only which of the two species the bee visited in the bouquet but also which of the two species the bee was coming from in the field before making its choice. Here the null hypothesis is that the plant species the bee chose in the bouquet does not depend on the species the bee was coming from in the field. To do this test of independence, we use the chi-squared statistic again, but this time to test a *2 x 2 contingency table.* A similar approach can evaluate Experiment 3(c).

Finally, to analyze Experiment 3(b), we can take several approaches. Although the numbers of probes are integer values, strictly speaking, they will have too large a range to be considered a separate category for an analysis of frequencies by the chi-squared test. We can either create a small number of categories (e.g., 0–5 probes, 5–10 probes, etc.) and use the chi-squared test, or we can simply treat the numbers of probes as continuous variables and use a t-test or a nonparametric equivalent such as a Mann-Whitney U-test. The latter is probably preferable because the numbers of probes are unlikely to meet the assumptions of normality.

Thought Questions

1. To stay constant on flower species A, a bee presumably will sometimes encounter but not visit another rewarding species B. Wouldn't it be more energetically efficient, in terms of food gain/travel time, for the bee to stop

and feed at B rather than to fly past it? Can constancy produce energy-efficient foraging? If not, why would we ever see animals doing it?

2. Why would a bee consistently prefer to visit one flower species over another?

3. If bees show preferences for certain flowers, do you think they are born with those preferences or acquire them through experience? Outline a set of experiments that would begin to answer this question.

4. If sprays of "pheromone" really produce a response in honeybees, would you expect a similar response in bumblebees? Why or why not? What sorts of functions have pheromone systems evolved to perform?

5. Experiment 3 is designed to show whether bees make predictions about the state of rewards they will find in the next flower they visit, based on their success or failure at finding rewards in the flower they just visited. Explain how you would interpret different possible experimental outcomes to draw conclusions about whether bees are in fact making such predictions or not.

6. The Laverty paper, which is relevant to question 1, contains some errors in data analysis that affect one of Laverty's conclusions. (He later published the appropriate corrections.) Track down these mistakes, fix them, and discuss the consequences for the message of the paper.

References

Bouquet-Choice Technique.

Thomson, J. D. 1981. Field measures of constancy in bumble bees. *American Midland Naturalist* 105:377–380.

Dependence of Foraging Decisions on Recent Experience (Experiment 3).

Taneyhill, D. 1994. Evolution of complex foraging behavior in bumble bees. Ph.D. diss., State University of New York–Stony Brook.

Thomson, J. D., W. P. Maddison, and R. C. Plowright. 1982. Behavior of bumble bee pollinators on *Aralia hispida* Vent. (Araliaceae). *Oecologia* 54:326–336.

Flower Constancy.

Chittka, L. and J. D. Thomson. 1997. Sensori-motor learning and its relevance for task specialization in bumble bees. *Behavioral Ecology and Sociobiology* 41:385–398.

Chittka, L., J. D. Thomson, and N. M. Waser. 1999. Flower constancy, insect psychology, and plant evolution. *Naturwissenschaften* 86:361–377.

Laverty, T. M. 1994. Costs to switching plant species. *Canadian Journal of Zoology* 72:43–47.

Waser, N. M. 1986. Flower constancy: Definition, cause and measurement. *American Naturalist* 127:593–603.

Wilson, P. W. and M. Stine. 1996. Floral constancy in bumble bees: Handling efficiency or perceptual conditioning? *Oecologia* 106:493–499.

Bees.

Heinrich, B. 1979. Bumblebee Economics. Belknap, Cambridge Massachusetts.

Prys-Jones, O. E. and S. A. Corbet. 1991. Bumblebees. *Naturalists' Handbooks* 6. 2d ed. Richmond, Slough, U.K.

OTHER PROJECTS

Rather than detailed descriptions, the following are general suggestions for projects, equipment, and approaches that can be developed into either class projects or individual research questions. A few references are given to provide entry into the literature. *Techniques for Pollination Biologists* (Kearns and Inouye 1993) gives detailed recipes for most of the necessary procedures.

Community Ecology

Within an area, the distribution of different bumblebee species across plant species has been thought to reflect differences in tongue length, so that long-tongued bees concentrate on long-tubed flowers, etc. (Inouye 1977, 1980; Pyke 1982). A class can collect bees (not only bumblebees) on a wide range of local plant species, sort the bees into species or at least "morphospecies," measure the tongue lengths of the various species (or extract them from the literature), measure the tube lengths of the plants, and search for the expected relationship. (Instructions for pinning and labeling insects for collections can be found in Kearns and Inouye [1993] and references therein. If possible, consult with a local entomologist for tips on proper pinning and storing of insects so that your collection will be of value to others). The primary data set, which is a matrix of plants by pollinators, is particularly well suited for ordination techniques (Ludwig and Reynolds 1988). The same data set can illuminate various aspects of biodiversity, including distributions of relative abundances and the calculation of species diversity, niche breadths, and niche overlaps. Curious students can examine aspects of the plants in addition to tube length, such as flower color, nectar production, and taxonomic identity, all of which might also influence the spectrum of visitors.

Pollen Input to a Colony

This requires an actively foraging colony, preferably located indoors with an entrance tunnel incorporating the "squeeze chute" pollen-catching device shown in Photograph 6-2. Simply watching the forager traffic can be very interesting. Foragers can be individually marked with paint marks or labels, and the times of their departures and returns noted. The colors and sizes of the pollen loads can be scored subjectively; different colors indicate different plant species. Changes through the day in load types or sizes per trip time give information on what individuals are doing and how successful they are. If one pollen becomes scarcer through the day, do bees respond by bringing back smaller loads, by taking longer to bring back the same-sized load, by switching to another species, by switching to nectar foraging, or by giving up foraging? Anyone interested in using bumblebees for crop pollination might want to look at pollen loads in this way to see if bumblebees are actually visiting the crop.

For more precise information, pollen pellets can be knocked from the corbiculae while the bee is caught in the squeeze chute, weighed if desired, and then examined both macroscopically and microscopically. Macroscopic analysis can reveal switches from one pollen to another in the middle of a foraging bout; the upper and lower portions of the pellet may be different colors (Photograph 7-2, page 112).

Microscopic analysis of pollen grains can identify different pollens, usually to plant family and often to genus, by the characteristic microsculpting of the outer walls or exines. To see these structures as clearly as possible, the grains should be subjected to a procedure called acetolysis (see Kearns and Inouye 1993), which uses harsh acids and bases to burn away everything but the highly resistant exines. Because acetolysis is time-consuming, somewhat dangerous, and requires a fume hood, we suggest a simpler alternative. Prepare glycerin jelly tinted with basic fuchsin stain using the recipe below:

175 cc	Distilled water
150 cc	Glycerin
50 g	Gelatin
5 g	Crystalline phenol
as desired	Crystalline basic fuchsin stain (also found in chemical supply catalogs as pararosaniline)

To make the jelly, add the gelatin to the distilled water in a beaker and heat until it is dissolved. Then add the glycerin and phenol and stir the mixture while warming it gently. Add basic fuchsin crystals to the mixture until the color approaches that of claret. The mixture should be filtered through glass wool into sterile containers, which should then be sealed. Phenol is added as a preservative, but it is also quite toxic to humans. Although it is probably essential in humid environments, in dry regions you might eliminate the phenol and refrigerate the final product (Beattie 1971; Kearns and Inouye 1993).

Place a small piece of the jelly on a microscope slide, add a small pollen sample, and heat the slide to melt—but not boil—the jelly. An alcohol lamp or a bare lightbulb will serve for heat. Press on a cover slip, let it cool, and you will have a semipermanent mount that shows most of the features of the grains. There are various manuals for identifying pollen grains (Faegri, Kaland, and Krzywinski 1989; see also references in Kearns and Inouye 1993), but these tend to feature scanning electron micrographs or pictures of acetolyzed grains. You will probably have better luck if you use the same glycerin jelly technique to make up a local reference collection of the plants in flower at the time. Even if you choose not to identify the grains collected by bees, it is still interesting to prepare some slides to examine the diversity of grains and to appreciate the ornamentation on these microscopic artworks. Recall that a pupal cell from an old bumblebee nest retains the exines of all the pollen fed to the bee. Such cells will yield this complete record after acetolysis.

Movement Patterns on Structured Inflorescences

Beginning with Pyke (1978 a and b), many observers have collected data on the "foraging rules" that bees use on vertical inflorescences. There has been much analysis relating those movement patterns to the nectar volumes in the flowers to determine if the bees are foraging optimally (see Best and Bierzychudek 1982; Pleasants 1989). Although these analyses can be rather arcane, simply establishing the rules (by repeatedly observing bees) constitutes a worthwhile investigation that will raise a number of questions. This exercise would be best suited for late summer or early fall when worker numbers are high. The basic questions are: Do bees tend to move up the stem, down the stem, or show no pattern? Say they tend to move up; do they start at the bottommost flower or somewhere higher? Do they depart from the topmost flower or somewhere lower? Do they miss flowers as they move along the stem? Do they ever revisit flowers? If they do revisit flowers, are they more likely to leave the inflorescence (see the paper by Thomson, Maddison, and Plowright [1982] cited in the interview bouquet exercise). Pyke noted that some plant species have orderly inflorescences where the flowers come off the stem in the same direction, whereas others have flowers sticking out in all directions. He proposed that the latter plants were adapted to confuse pollinators into revisiting flowers and then leaving prematurely. If these plants were not confusing, bees would systematically visit all the flowers, which would increase the amount of undesirable within-plant pollination. Confused bees should cause more outcross pollination. Several aspects of Pyke's conjecture can be tested by simple experiments. Galen and Plowright (1985) showed that nectar-collecting and pollen-collecting bees on fireweed (*Epilobium angustifolium*) have somewhat different patterns that seem well suited to the different vertical distributions of these rewards.

Flight Distances and Rewards

Pyke (1978b) proposed that bumblebees ought to fly shorter distances and turn more sharply after receiving good rewards at a plant. If they encountered an empty plant, they would do better to make longer, straighter flights before feeding again. The rationale is that standing crops of nectar in a plant population would be patchy in space: they would be low where a bee had recently drained them by systematic foraging, and high in areas that had not recently been visited. By showing "area-restricted search," bees would move quickly through poor patches but linger in rich patches, thereby increasing their energy intake per unit time. A simple test of this proposition rests on the assumption (which has been confirmed in several situations) that the amount of time a bee spends at a flower is directly related to how much reward it gets there. Therefore one can look for area-restricted foraging by correlating the time a bee spends at a plant or flower with the distance it flies to its next stop. Note that you can easily get a spurious correlation if you pool data from many bees. If some bees are sick, or old with tattered wings, they may tend to fly short distances and work slowly (Thomson, Maddison, and Plowright 1982). Therefore it is ideal to follow each individual as long as possible so that data can be analyzed within individuals. Such an exercise can be a good demonstration of the danger of spurious correlation.

Trapline Foraging and Use of Space

The prediction that bees should show "area-restricted search" presupposes that the bees are searching for good places to feed. Another possibility is that individual bees may have already established foraging areas to which they return repeatedly. An extreme version of site fidelity is traplining, in which a forager may repeatedly visit a set of plants in a particular order, just as a fur trapper will check a trapline to see whether anything has been caught. In such a case, how far the forager flies may be unrelated to the reward it has just received. Bumblebee workers do show tendencies to trapline, at least on certain plants that present rapidly renewing floral rewards (Manning 1956; Thomson, Maddison, and Plowright 1982; Thomson 1996). One illuminating exercise is to set up shop in a stand of plants that receives high visitation, mark bees individually, and keep track of how many are seen again. Are some individuals sighted again and again? If so, bees are at least maintaining individual foraging areas rather than searching widely. The next step could be following some of these individuals for as long as possible and see whether they frequently retrace their steps within their areas. This might entail labeling and mapping the plant population. Although a rigorous statistical demonstration of traplining is data-intensive and computationally forbidding (Thomson, Slatkin, and Thomson 1997), it is not difficult to develop an intuitive sense of whether or not a followed bee is familiar with the plants it is working. Simple experiments include removing traplined plants and observing the bees' reactions (Manning 1956), and arraying potted plants to train bees to develop particular flight paths, then changing the array to gauge the persistence of the trapline (Thomson 1996).

By concentrating on a single plant in a population that is being traplined by marked bees, one can obtain histories of the visits by particular bees. Williams and Thomson (1998) videotaped a plant of *Penstemon strictus* for a single day, discovering that 57 percent of the 553 visits to the plant were made by only four bumblebees, which were returning at approximately seven-minute intervals. Such foraging is quite different from that envisioned by the early "optimal search" models, which considered short time scales only and assumed that bees should avoid revisiting a plant. Unfortunately, most consumer-grade video cameras are incapable of reliably revealing bees' color marks, so it is necessary for an observer to narrate a continuous play-by-play account on the audio track. The burden of transcribing videotape is so great that we could not recommend this approach to any but the most dedicated student, but one need not have records of each flower visit to achieve some insights. Sitting by a plant with a stopwatch and a notepad can be quite instructive, if the visitation rate is high enough. A simple voice recorder is the next step up. Sarah Corbet (personal communication) has used a cheap printing calculator to record the times of visits, linking this record to the tape-recorded voice record by writing numbers on the printed times periodically or by saying the time.

Flight Cages and Arenas

Although much can be done with observing bees outdoors, greater refinement and experimental control can be achieved by confining bees to a cage or an arena in which the investigator can set conditions. Although the idea of entering a cage full of bees sounds intimidating, it need not be. Even if you wish to do an experiment in which an entire colony forages within a cage, recall that only a small fraction of the workers are likely to be out foraging, and that they will be concentrating on finding food. Tomato growers routinely work in greenhouses alongside their bees. Still, you should observe precautions: avoid cage work with any of the *Fervidobombus* species, which are vicious; keep your colony small; wear light-colored clothing with long sleeves; add a head net for maximum protection; have nets and jars at hand; and make sure that the colony box is securely mounted in a place where it cannot be kicked or jostled. If possible, place the colony outside the cage and let the bees enter only through a tunnel that can easily be closed off. As a final drastic measure, you may wish to obtain one of the specialized spray cans of insecticide that are sold for rapid knockdown of hornets' nests and the like. We have never used one of these on bumblebees, but it could be useful in the event of an overturned nest box of irate bees.

For many flight-cage experiments, you need not release a whole colony. Instead you can use a gated entrance tunnel to let out only one or a few workers at a time. You may in fact not need a colony at all; wild-caught bees can be introduced singly for many purposes, although you may need to coax them to feed.

If you need a large cage, BioQuip sells some specifically designed for insects, but a less expensive screened tent or lawn "gazebo" will suffice. A plain interior room can serve as a flight cage if you scrupulously find and plug all holes or crevices where bees can disappear. The principal difficulty in using flight cages is getting the bees to behave normally. Although some workers may settle down easily to their assigned tasks, others will fly to the sunniest upper corner and remain there. If your colony is large enough, you may wish to ignore these intransigent bees. If you need to spur them into action, however, you can catch them in vials and return them to the hive, flick them off the screen into flight, or shove flowers into their faces to try to get them to feed, then gently bring the flower with the feeding bee down toward your experimental setup.

For many experimental purposes, small flight arenas are better than flight cages. We have built a variety of these for particular purposes. The common elements are usually a plywood box, a clear plastic lid or viewing window, and some means for reaching in to adjust apparatus, for removing bees, etc. We have successfully provided access by cutting a broad opening in the plywood, gluing a piece of 1-inch-thick polyurethane foam sheet over the opening, then cutting a horizontal slit in the foam. As in a glove box, you can insert one or both arms through the slit to work inside the box. Although the foam provides only an imperfect seal, it is quite sufficient if you are working with a single bee and watching it continuously. The foam will not lock workers in the arena if you are not there to police the opening, so you need to provide a solid cover for the access hatch if you will be leaving bees in the arena between sessions.

Experiments suited for flight cages include the following:

1. Any of the foraging experiments described already. They can be refined by using artificial flowers (next paragraph) so that you know what rewards the bees have encountered. We have mentioned how Waddington and Heinrich (1979) clarified whether or not bees went upward on vertical inflorescences because they were following a nectar gradient.

2. Any experiment that requires repeated testing of individuals with known histories, such as Laverty's (1980, 1994) elegant experiments on how bees learn to handle complex flowers. Starting with callow, therefore naive, bees, Laverty observed and videotaped individuals

trying to handle different sorts of flowers ranging from simple to complex. He showed how the frequency of mistakes declined with experience.

3. Experiments that require special preparation of real flowers, such as removing the anthers of a series of recipient flowers to see how far bees carry pollen from a particular donor flower ("pollen carryover"; e.g., Thomson 1986; Morris et al. 1994).

4. Experiments that require unusual conditions. Collett, Fry, and Wehner (1993) used compartments in a cage to control honeybees' access to visual landmarks. Chittka, Williams, Rasmussen, and Thomson (1998) used a rotating circular arena (and infrared video) to examine how bumblebees orient in complete darkness. This could not have been done in the field. Cages are also useful for mating bees as part of a rearing program or for encouraging queens to start nesting.

Artificial flowers. Bumblebees can be trained to drink nectar from a variety of artificial flowers. Although Brian (1957) successfully induced them to visit waxed-paper flowers outdoors, most experimenters have worked in enclosures, where competition from real flowers is absent. To create spatial arrays of flowers, Waddington (1980) and Real (1981) used large sheets of Plexiglas acrylic with grids of shallow wells drilled into the plastic. A cheaper option is to cut Plexiglas into small tiles about 1 inch square, drill wells in them, and then distribute the tiles as desired on plywood or cardboard sheets. Using small tiles makes it easy to use a drill press to standardize the depth of the wells. Holes of $3/32$-inch diameter work well. Colorful "corollas" can be applied to the tiles with paint or bits of plastic tape. Alternatively, use a color printer to print realistic flowers on paper that can be placed underneath the transparent tiles. Nectar can be supplied to the wells by a small pipette. For repeated dispensing of known volumes of solution, automated pipetting devices are best. The battery-powered Rainin EDP-2 (Rainin Instrument, Woburn, MA), for example, can dispense aliquots as small as 1 microliter, which is a realistic range for many real flowers. We use an EDP-2 fitted with a blunted hypodermic needle (which fills wells more easily than the standard plastic tip), and a small DC power source to eliminate dependence on expensive lithium batteries.

Tiles can be grouped to create various arrangements such as vertical "inflorescences," or different shapes of plastic can be drilled in various patterns for particular experiments. For example, Taneyhill and Thomson (unpublished) used equilateral triangles of plastic with a circle of wells in each corner to further explore the *Aralia* results found by Thomson, Maddison, and Plowright (1982). Kipp, Knight, and Kipp (1989) investigated turning angles with a clever design of artificial flowers.

Although welled flowers are easy to build, the required manual refilling is tedious and prevents certain desirable designs. Various Rube Goldberg designs have been developed to refill flowers automatically. The most sophisticated have used power-driven syringes or even automotive fuel injectors. We suggest two simpler and cheaper designs. Hartling and Plowright (1979) provide drawings for a solenoid-base flower that refills when an electromagnet is energized by dipping a short length of fine glass tubing into a protected reservoir. The tube fills by capillary action. Thomson (unpublished) has devised a relatively foolproof flower that secretes continuously. A simple pipette, which serves as the nectar reservoir, hangs tip-down by a thread wrapped around the shaft of a low-speed electric motor. The pipette's tip plugs into one end of a length of flexible Tygon tubing; the other end of the tubing loops upward to plug into the bottom of a plastic flower tile. As the motor turns, the reservoir rises slowly and nectar oozes out at the flower end at a rate determined by the speed of the motor, the diameter of the shaft, and the cross-sectional area of the reservoir. We plan to use this design to study traplining in large cages.

Artificial flowers can also be set up to record data electronically. Chittka and Thomson (1997) used infrared-emitting and infrared-sensing diodes to record bumblebee visits to artificial flowers built as T-mazes. Wired to an interface board in a personal computer, this system automatically wrote the timing data to a disk file. In the tradition of Skinner boxes, the design of artificial flowers gives great scope for tinkerers to devise clever new mechanical and electronic solutions.

Appendix 1

Sources of Information

Web Sites

http://www.earthlife.net/insects/six.html
UK bees. Gordon Ramel

http://www.evergreen.edu/user/serv_res/research/arthropod/ TESCBiota/
Apidae/BOMBUS/biology.htm
US, Matthew Kweskin

http://ourworld.compuserve.com/homepages/kbservices/BUMBLE.HTM
US, David Kendall

http://www.mearns.org.uk/mrssmith/bees/bees.htm
Scotland, Laura Smith

http://www.anet-chi.com/~manytimes/page31.htm
plants for bumblebees, nest box construction; Conrad A. Berube

http://www.seliyahu.org.il/eBees.htm
commercial supplier in Israel

http://www.cae.wisc.edu/~oliphant/bees/bombus/
Wisconsin, US, Paul Oliphant

http://www.koppert.nl/e003.shtml
Koppert, commercial supplier, the Netherlands

http://indecol.mtroyal.ab.ca/bumble/
Robin Owen, Canadian bumblebees (most overlap with US)

Web Sites on Bees and Other Pollinators

http://www.loganbeelab.usu.edu/
Utah State University, Bee biology and systematics lab

http://www.desert.net/museum/fp/pollination.html
Arizona-Sonora desert museum

http://198.22.133.109/na/bgardn.html
Steve Buchmann, planting a bee garden

http://www.anet-chi.com/%7Emanytimes/page29.htm
native bee resources, Tom Clothier

http://www.pollinatorparadise.com
 Karen Strickler, solitary bees and pollination information
http://www.cf.ac.uk/ibra/index.shtml
 International Bee Research Association

LIST SERVERS

Bombus-l: An e-mail group devoted to conversation about bumblebees.
 To subscribe send message to: listserv@umdd.umd.edu
 text of message should say: subscribe bombus-l YOUR NAME

Apoidea: This e-mail group considers all bees, not just bumblebees.
 To subscribe send message to: macjordomo@biology.usu.edu
 text of message should say: SUBSCRIBE apoidea YOUR NAME

Appendix 2 ─────────

Suppliers

Opalith-Plättchen Bee Labels

Manufacturer:
Chr.Graze KG
Fabrik für Bienenzuchtgerate
7056 Weinstadt-Endersbach
Stuttgart, Germany
Telephone: (0 71 51) 6 11 47
Fax: 7151-609239

Retail Distributors:
Gustav Nenninger
8741 Saal A. Saale
Germany

Bienen Mathys AG
3762 Erlenbach i. S.
Switzerland

Epipen (treatment for anaphylactic shock due to bee sting)

http://www.deyinc.com/patientallergy.html
http://www.cgi.cadvision.com/~allergy/marketplace.html#allerex

Pollen for Feeding Bees

Local honeybee keepers may be able to supply you with pollen. If not, you might try purchasing frozen pollen from one of these sources:

Firm Yield Pollen Services, Inc.
301 N. 1st Avenue
Yakima, WA 98902
Telephone: 800-322-8852, 509-452-8063
Fax: 509-453-6838
E-mail: neil@firmanpollen.co
Web site: www.firmanpollen.com/

CC Pollen Co. (in 55-pound drums)
3627 E. Indian School Road, #209
Phoenix, AZ 85018-5126
Telephone: 800-875-0096
Web site: www.ccpollen.com/

Bumblebee Colony Distributors

Biobest

www.biobest.be/index_eng.htm

Biobest Canada Ltd.
2020 Mersea Road #3
RR 4, Township of Mersea
Leamington, Ontario N8H 3V7
Telephone: +1 519 322.21.78
Fax: +1 519 322.12.71
E-mail: biobest@wincom.net

International Technology Services
P.O. Box 75
Lafayette, CO 80026
Telephone: 303-661-9546
Fax: 303-661-9543

Koppert

Website: www.koppert.nl/e003.shtml

Koppert Biological System, Inc.
28465 Beverly Road
Romulus, MI 48174
Telephone: +1 734641 3763
Fax: +1 734641 3793

Koppert Canada Limited
3 Pullman Court
Scarborough, Ontario M1X 1E4
Telephone: +1 416 291 0040
Fax: +1 416 291 0902

Koppert Mexico S. A. de C.V.
Andromeda 47
Col. Prado Churubusco
Telephone: + 525 5399 888
Fax: + 525 5325 900

Appendix 3 ──────────

Photographic Field Guide to the Bumblebees of North America

These images of North American bumblebees include some of our own specimens, but most are from the Museum of Comparative Zoology at Harvard University and the American Museum of Natural History in New York. We thank the curators of both institutions for their help. Although some of the specimens are quite old, both collections had been recently curated. Therefore the identifications are as reliable as possible, even if some of the rarer specimens are a little battered. The photos were made on Fujichrome Velvia 35mm film using a ringflash. The images were scanned and edited digitally by the University Press of Colorado to remove pins, stray shadows, and the like.

In using these pictures to identify bees, readers must be careful in interpreting colors. First, there are always problems in reproducing colors perfectly. More important in this case is the tendency of insect colors to change after killing and during long exposure to fumigating chemicals in storage. In particular, light bright lemony yellows darken to ocher tones, and red-orange hues tend toward browns. Therefore, fresh specimens will tend to be brighter than any of the insects pictured here, and you will not be able to simply choose the closest color match. Instead you must look at the patterns of hairs on different segments and parts of the body, with the most important distinction being black versus light. Also look at hair length, from shaggy to sleek, and face shape, from long to short. Do not pay attention to posture; this depends on the vagaries of pinning and preservation.

Recall, of course, that most species show some variation in coloration, so your specimen of a particular species may not match the one we show. We have tried to select the most common coat-color variants, but you will need to consult more advanced technical keys for descriptions of the range of color variation. Space and cost limitations prevent us from presenting several angles for each specimen. We have compromised by showing queens both head-on (to show face length) and from a rear three-quarters angle (to capture the colors of the abdominal segments, which will probably be the characters you can most easily see in the field). For males, we show lateral views only. All pictures are to the same scale.

Range maps present very broad regional areas. For more detailed range information, see Table 1-1.

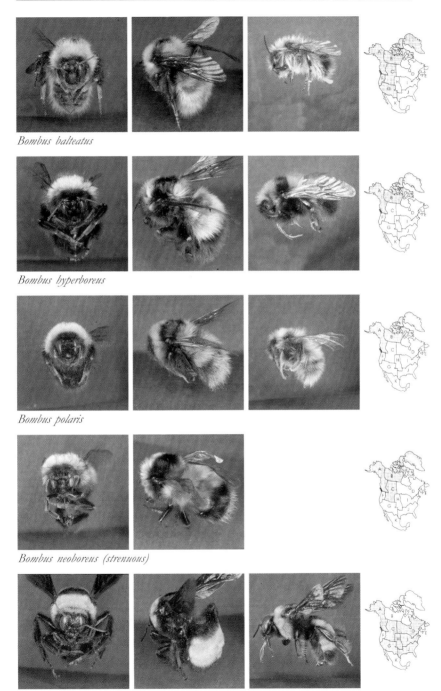

Bombus balteatus

Bombus hyperboreus

Bombus polaris

Bombus neoboreus (strenuous)

Bombus auricomus

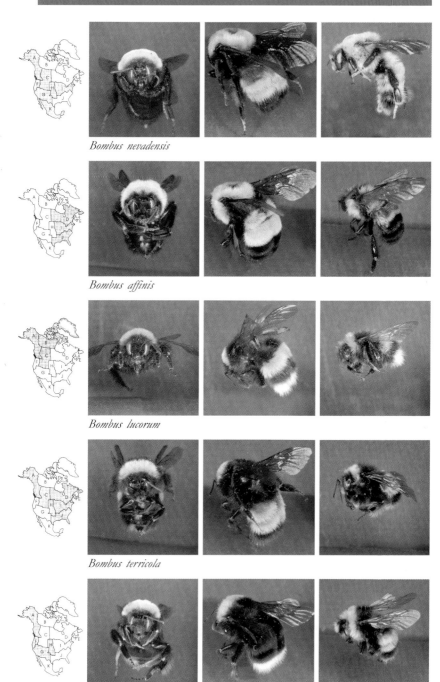

Bombus nevadensis

Bombus affinis

Bombus lucorum

Bombus terricola

Bombus terricola (occidentalis)

Bombus franklini

Bombus crotchii

Bombus rufocinctus

Bombus fervidus (californicus)

Bombus fervidus (fervidus)

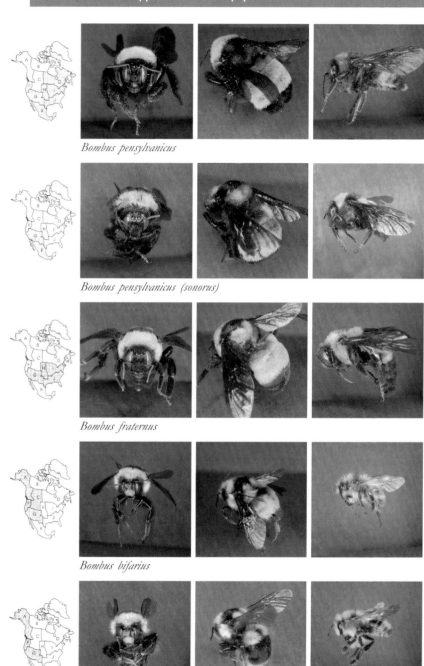

Bombus pensylvanicus

Bombus pensylvanicus (sonorus)

Bombus fraternus

Bombus bifarius

Bombus bifarius nearcticus

Bombus bimaculatus

  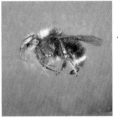

Bombus caliginosus

Bombus centralis

Bombus melanopygus (edwardsii)

Bombus flavifrons

Bombus flavifrons (dimidiatus)

Bombus frigidus

Bombus huntii

Bombus impatiens

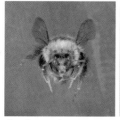

Bombus melanopygus

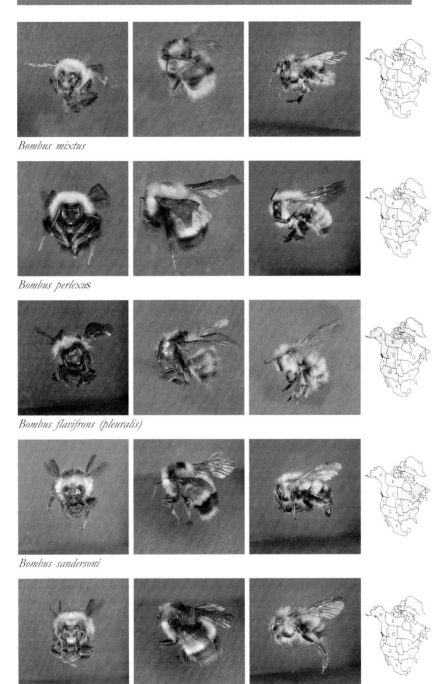

Bombus mixtus

Bombus perlexus

Bombus flavifrons (pleuralis)

Bombus sandersoni

Bombus sitkensis

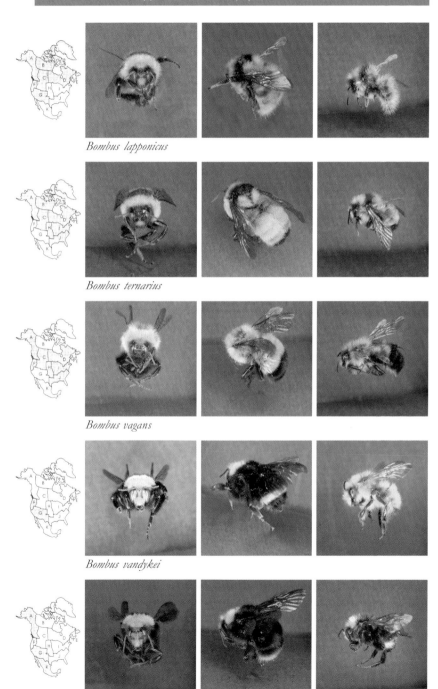

Bombus lapponicus

Bombus ternarius

Bombus vagans

Bombus vandykei

Bombus vosnesenskii

Bombus griseocollis

Bombus morrisoni

Bombus appositus

Bombus borealis

Psithyrus ashtoni

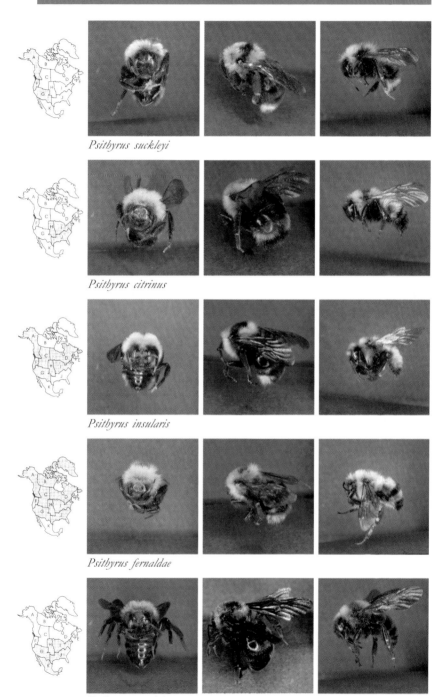

Psithyrus suckleyi

Psithyrus citrinus

Psithyrus insularis

Psithyrus fernaldae

Psithyrus variabilis

Photograph 1-1: The male (left) and the much larger queen of Bombus impatiens. *Note the stinger on the female. (The stinger is often not visible.)*

Photograph 1-2: Face view of Bombus impatiens *male (left) and queen. Note the yellower, hairier face of the male. Males tend to have longer fur and to be more yellow than females.*

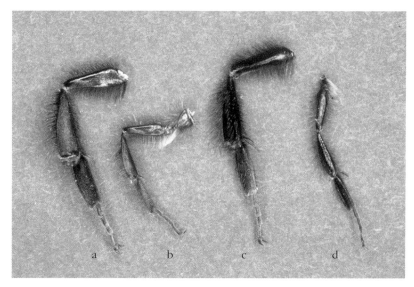

a   b   c   d

Photograph 1-3: Hind legs of female (a and c) and male (b and d) bumble-bees. Note the hairless corbicula in a. Females pack pollen loads into this concave, hairless surface.

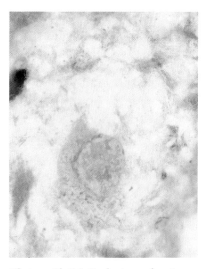

Photograph 2-1: Early stage of nest con-struction—this pollen lump has been chewed and sculpted by the queen.

Photograph 2-2: Nest in early stage of development. The wax honey pot on the left will store nectar. Addi-tional wax construction has occurred on the upper right. The pollen lump (lower left) is now ready and the queen will soon lay eggs.

Photograph 2-3: The queen lies on the incubation groove, regulating brood temperature.

Photograph 2-4a: The brood clump now contains first-brood larvae. A wax cell on top of the brood clump has been prepared for a second-brood egg. The incubation groove runs across the clump toward the honey pot.

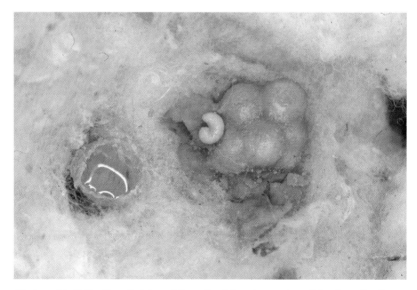

Photograph 2-4b: One first-brood larval cell has been opened to show the larva.

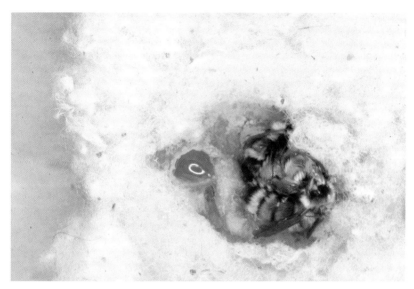

Photograph 2-5: The queen and two first-brood workers sit in the nest. Note the whitish "callow" coloration of the upper worker.

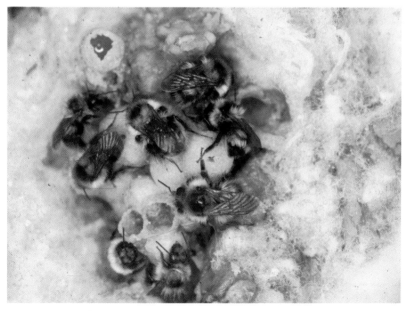

Photograph 2-6: The colony grows outward and upward in layers as the queen attaches new structures to old structures. Empty cocoons are modified with wax to create storage vessels for pollen and nectar.

Photograph 4-1: This asilid fly with its beelike appearance is actually a bee predator—an example of aggressive mimicry.

Photographs 4-2(a) and (b): Many species of flower-loving syrphid flies mimic bees. Although these flies cannot sting, they are probably shunned by predators that have learned from experience to avoid bees.

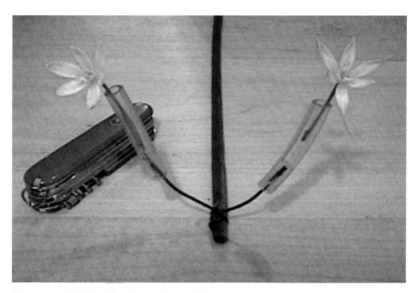

Photograph 7-1: The interview stick.

Photograph 7-2: This Bombus bifarius *worker carries a mixed pollen load. The orange pollen that was collected first is from lupines, and the whitish yellow pollen is from the penstemon flowers the bee is visiting now.*

References

Alford, D. V. 1975. *Bumblebees*. Davis-Poynter, London, U.K. 352 pp.

Arretz, P. V. and R. P. Macfarlane. 1986. The introduction of *Bombus ruderatus* to Chile for red clover pollination. *Bee World* 67:15–22.

Asada, S. and M. Ono. 1996. Crop pollination by Japanese bumblebees, *Bombus* spp. (Hymenoptera: Apidae): Tomato foraging behavior and pollination efficiency. *Applied Entomology and Zoology* 31:581–586.

Beattie, A. J. 1971. A technique for the study of insect-borne pollen. *Pan-Pacific Entomologist* 47:82.

Best, L. S., and P. Bierzychudek. 1982. Pollinator foraging on foxglove: A test of a new model. *Evolution* 36:70–79.

Bowlin, R. W., V. J. Tepedino, and T. L. Griswold. 1993. The reproductive biology of *Eriogonum pelinophilum* (Polygonaceae). In *Proceedings Southwestern Rare and Endangered Plant Conference*. R. Sivinski and K. Lightfoot, eds. New Mexico Forestry and Resources Conservation Division, Miscellaneous Publication Number 2. Santa Fe, New Mexico. pp. 296–302.

Brian, A. D. 1951 (Cited in Wilson 1971). Brood development in *Bombus agrorum* (Hymenoptera, Bombidae). *Entomologists' Monthly Magazine* 87:207–212.

Brian, A. D. 1952 (cited in Müller et al. 1992). Division of labour and foraging in *Bombus agrorum* Fabricius. *Journal of Animal Ecology* 21:223–240.

Brian, A. D. 1957. Differences in the flowers visited by four species of bumble-bees and their causes. *Journal of Animal Ecology* 26:71–98.

Buchmann, S. L. 1983. Buzz pollination in angiosperms. Pp. 73–113 in C. E. Jones, and R. J. Little, eds. *Handbook of Experimental Pollination Biology*, Van Nostrand Reinhold, New York.

Buchmann, S. L. and G. P. Nabhan. 1996. *The Forgotten Pollinators*. Island Press, Washington D.C. 292 pp.

Chittka, L. and J. D. Thomson. 1997. Sensori-motor learning and its relevance for task specialization in bumble bees. *Behavioral Ecology and Sociobiology* 41:385–398.

Chittka, L., J. D. Thomson, and N. M. Waser. 1999. Flower constancy, insect psychology, and plant evolution. *Naturwissenschaften* 86:361–377.

Chittka, L., N. Williams, H. Rasmussen, and J. D. Thomson. 1998. Navigation without vision: bumble bee orientation in complete darkness. *Proceeding of the Royal Society of London* B 265:1–6.

Collett, T. S., S. N. Fry, and R. Wehner. 1993. Sequence learning by honeybees. *Journal of Comparative Physiology* 172:693–706.

Cumber, R. A. 1953. Some aspects of the biology and ecology of humble-bees bearing upon the yields of red-clover seed in New Zealand. *N. Z. J. Sci. Tech.* 34:227–240.

Darwin, C. R. (1859) 1964. *On the Origin of Species by Means of Natural Selection*. A facsimile of the first edition. Harvard University Press, Cambridge, Massachusetts. pp. 74, 236–237.

Darwin, C. R. (1878) 1989. *The Effects of Cross and Self Fertilization in the Vegetable Kingdom.* The works of Charles Darwin, vol. 25. P. H. Barrett and R. B. Freeman, eds. New York University Press, New York. 405 pp.

Day, M. C. 1991. *Towards the Conservation of Aculeate Hymenoptera in Europe.* Council of Europe, Strasbourg, France.

de Ruijter, A. 1997. Commercial bumblebee rearing and its implications. *Acta Horticulturae* 437:261–269.

Delaplane, K. S. 1995a. Bumble beekeeping: The queen starter box. *American Bee Journal* 135:743–745.

Delaplane, K. S. 1995b. Why bumble bees? *American Bee Journal* 135:459–460.

Delaplane, K. S. 1996a. Bumble beekeeping: Inducing queens to nest in captivity. *American Bee Journal* 136:42–43.

Delaplane, K. S. 1996b. Bumble beekeeping: Handling mature colonies, mating queens. *American Bee Journal* 136:105–106.

Donovan, B. J. 1990. Selection and importation of new pollinators to New Zealand. *The New Zealand Entomologist* 13:26–32.

Dornhaus, A. and L. Chittka. 1999. Evolutionary origins of bee dances. *Nature* 401:38.

Dramstad, W. E. 1996. Do bumblebees (Hymenoptera:Apidae) really forage close to their nests? *Journal of Insect Behavior* 9(2):163–182.

Dramstad, W. and G. Fry. 1995. Foraging activity of bumblebees (*Bombus*) in relation to flower resources on arable land. *Agriculture, Ecosystems and Environment* 53:123–135.

Evans, H. E. and K. M. O'Neill. 1988. *The Natural History and Behavior of North American Beewolves.* Comstock Pub. Associates, Ithaca, New York. 278 pp.

Faegri K., P. E. Kaland, and K. Krzywinski. 1989. *Textbook of Pollen Analysis.* 4th ed. John Wiley and Sons, New York.

Franklin, H. J. 1912. The Bombidae of the New World. *Transactions American Entomological Society* 38:177–486.

Free, J. B. 1987. *Pheromones of Social Bees.* Chapman and Hall, London, U.K. 218 pp.

Free, J. B. and Butler, C. G. 1959. *Bumblebees*. Collins, London, U.K.

Freeman, R. B. 1968. Charles Darwin on the routes of male humble bees. *Bull. Br. Mus. Nat. Hist. Hist. Ser.* 3:177–189.

Frison, T. H. 1927. Records and descriptions of Western Bumblebees. (Bremidae). *Proceedings of the California Academy of Sciences* 16(12):365–380.

Fussell, M. and S. A. Corbet. 1992. Flower usage by bumble-bees: A basis for forage plant management. *Journal of Applied Ecology* 29:451–465.

Galen, C., and R. C. Plowright. 1985. The effects of nectar level and flower development on pollen carry-over in inflorescences of fireweed (*Epilobium angustifolium*) (Onagraceae). *Canadian Journal of Botany* 63:488–491.

Gauld, I. D., N. M. Collins, M. G. Fitton. 1990. *The Biological Significance and Conservation of Hymenoptera in Europe*. Council of Europe, Strasbourg, France. 47 pp.

Gess, F. W. and S. K. Gess. 1993. Effects of increasing land utilization on species representation and diversity of aculeate wasps and bees in the semi-arid areas of Southern Africa. Pp. 83–113 in *Hymenoptera and Biodiversity*, J. LaSalle and I. D. Gauld, eds., CAB International, Wallingford, U.K.

Goulson, D., S. A. Hawson, and J. C. Stout. 1998. Foraging bumblebees avoid flowers already visited by conspecifics or by other bumblebee species. *Animal Behaviour* 55:199–206.

Gwynne, D. T. 1981. Nesting biology of the bumblebee wolf *Philanthus bicinctus* Mickel. (Hymenoptera, Sphecidae). *American Midland Naturalist* 105:130–138.

Hamilton, W. D. 1972. Altruism and related phenomena, mainly in the social insects. *Annual Review Ecology and Systematics* 3:193–232.

Hanson, P. E. and I. D. Gauld 1995. *The Hymenoptera of Costa Rica*. Oxford University Press, New York. 893 pp.

Harder, L. D. 1986. Influences on the density and dispersion of bumble bee nests (Hymenoptera: Apidae). *Holarctic Ecology* 9:99–103.

Hartling, L. K., and R. C. Plowright, 1979. Foraging by bumble bees on patches of artificial flowers: A laboratory study. *Canadian Journal of Zoology* 57:1866–1970.

Heinrich, B. 1976. The foraging specializations of individual bumblebees. *Ecological Monographs* 46:105–128.

Heinrich, B. 1979. *Bumblebee Economics*. Harvard University Press, Cambridge, Massachusetts. 248 pp.

Heinrich, B. 1993. *The Hot-Blooded Insects*. Harvard University Press, Cambridge, Massachusetts. 601 pp.

Herrera, C. M. 1990. Bumble bees feeding on non-plant food sources. *Bee World* 71(2):67–69.

Hobbes, G.A. 1964. Ecology of species of *Bombus* Latr. (Hymenoptera: Apidae) in southern Alberta. I. Subgenus *Alpinobombus*. *Canadian Entomologist* 96:1465–1470.

Hobbes, G. A. 1965. Ecology of species of *Bombus* Latr. (Hymenoptera: Apidae) in southern Alberta. II. Subgenus *Bombias* Robt. *Canadian Entomologist* 97:120–128.

Hobbes, G. A. 1965. Ecology of species of *Bombus* Latr. (Hymenoptera: Apidae) in southern Alberta. III. Subgenus *Cullumanobombus* Vogt. *Canadian Entomologist* 97:1293–1302.

Hobbes, G. A. 1966. Ecology of species of *Bombus* Latr. (Hymenoptera: Apidae) in southern Alberta. IV. Subgenus *Fervidobombus* (Skorikov). *Canadian Entomologist* 98:33–39.

Hobbes, G. A. 1966. Ecology of species of *Bombus* Latr. (Hymenoptera: Apidae) in southern Alberta. V. Subgenus *Subterraneobombus* Vogt. *Canadian Entomologist* 98:288–294.

Hobbes, G. A. 1967. Ecology of species of *Bombus* Latr. (Hymenoptera: Apidae) in southern Alberta. VI. Subgenus *Pyrobombus*. *Canadian Entomologist* 99:1271–1292.

Hughes, M. H. 1996. Commercial rearing of bumble bees. In *Bumble Bees for Pleasure and Profit*. A. Matheson, ed. International Bee Research Association, Cardiff, U.K.

Inouye, D. W. 1977. Species structure of bumblebee communities in North America and Europe. Pp. 35–40 in *The Role of Arthropods in Forest Ecosystems*. W. J. Mattson, ed. Springer Verlag, New York.

Inouye, D. W. 1978. Resource partitioning in bumblebee guilds: Experimental studies of foraging behavior. *Ecology* 59:672–678.

Inouye, D. W. 1980. The effect of proboscis and corolla tube lengths on patterns and rates of flower visitation by bumblebees. *Oecologia* 45:197–201.

Inouye, D. W. 1982. The ecology of nectar robbing. In *The Biology of Nectaries*. T. S. Elias and B. L. Bentley, eds. Columbia University Press, New York.

Ito, M. 1985. Supraspecific classification of bumblebees based on the characters of male genitalia. *Contributions from the Institute of Low Temperature Science, Series B*, Volume 20. 143 pp.

Kearns, C. A., and D. W. Inouye. 1993. *Techniques for Pollination Biologists*. University Press of Colorado, Boulder. 583 pp.

Kearns, C. A., D. W. Inouye, and N. M. Waser. 1998. Endangered mutualisms: The conservation of plant-pollinator interactions. *Annual Review of Ecology and Systematics* 29:83–112.

Kevan, P. G. 1974. Pollination, pesticides, and environmental quality [letter]. *BioScience* 24: 198–199.

Kevan P. G. 1975a. Forest application of the insecticide Fenitrothion and its effect on wild bee pollinators (Hymenoptera: Apoidea) of lowbush blueberries (*Vaccinium* spp.) in southern New Brunswick, Canada. *Biol. Conserv.* 7:301–309.

Kevan P. G. 1975b. Pollination and environmental conservation. *Environmental Conservation* 2:293–298.

Kevan P. G. 1991. Pollination: Keystone process in sustainable global productivity. *Acta Hortic.* 288:103–109.

Kevan, P. G. 1998. Pollinators in agroecosystems: Their keystone role in sustainable productivity and bioindication. In *Biodiversity in Agroecosystems Role of Sustainability and Bioindication*. M. Paoletti, ed. Elsevier, New York.

Kevan, P. G. and R. C. Plowright. 1989. Fenitrothion and insect pollination. In *Environmental Effects of Fenitrothion Use in Forestry: Impacts on Insect Pollinators, Songbirds, and Aquatic Organisms*. W. R. Ernst, P. A. Pearce, and T. L. Pollock, eds. Environ. Canada, Dartmouth, Nova Scotia. pp. 13–42.

Kevan, P. G., E. A. Clark, and F. G. Thomas. 1990. Pollination: A crucial ecological and mutualistic link in agroforestry and sustainable agriculture. *Proc. Entomol. Soc. Ontario* 121:43–48.

Kipp, L. R., W. Knight, and E. R. Kipp. 1989. Influence of resource topography on pollinator flight directionality of two species of bees. *Journal of Insect Behaviour* 2:453–472.

Knuth, P. 1906–1909. *Handbook of Flower Pollination Based on Hermann Müller's Work* The Fertilisation of Flowers by Insects. 3 volumes. Clarendon Press, Oxford.

Krombein K. V., P. D. Hurd Jr., D. R. Smith, and B. D. Burks. 1979. *Catalog of Hymenoptera in America North of Mexico*. Vol. 2 Apocrita (Aculeata). Smithsonian Institution Press, Washington, D.C. pp. 2191–2207.

Kwak, M. M., P. Kremer, E. Boerrichter, and C. van den Brand. 1991. Pollination of the rare species *Phyteuma nigrum* (Campanulaceae): Flight distances of bumble-bees. *Proc. Exp. Appl. Entomol.* 2:131–136.

Labougle, J. M. 1990. *Bombus* of Mexico and Central America (Hymenoptera, Apidae). *U. Kansas Science Bull.* 54:(3):35–73.

Laverty, T. M. 1980. The flower-visiting behavior of bumble bees-floral complexity and learning. *Canadian Journal of Zoology* 58:1324–1335.

Laverty, T. M. 1994. Costs to switching plant species. *Canadian Journal of Zoology* 72:43–47.

Laverty, T. M. and R. C. Plowright. 1988. Flower handling by bumblebees: A comparison of specialists and generalists. *Animal Behaviour* 36:733–740.

Ludwig, J. A. and J. R. Reynolds. 1988. *Statistical Ecology*. Wiley-Interscience, New York. 337 pp.

Macior, L. W. 1978. Pollination ecology of vernal angiosperms. *Oikos* 30:452–460

Manning, A. 1956. Some aspects of the foraging behaviour of bumble-bees. *Behaviour* 9:164–201.

Matheson, A. 1996. *Bumble Bees for Pleasure and Profit*. International Bee Research Association, Cardiff, U.K. 47 pp.

Michener, C. D. 1974. *The Social Behavior of Bees*. Harvard University Press, Cambridge, Massachusetts. 404 pp.

Michener, C. D. 2000. *The Bees of the World*. Johns Hopkins University Press, Baltimore, Maryland. 950pp.

Michener, C. D., R. J. McGinley, and B. N. Danforth. 1994. *The Bee Genera of North and Central America (Hymenoptera: Apoidea)*. Smithsonian Institution Press, Washington, D.C. 209 pp.

Milliron, H. E. 1971–1973. A Monograph of the Western Hemisphere Bumblebees (Hymenoptera: Apidae; Bombinae). *Memoirs of the Entomological Society of Canada*. (Ottawa, Canada.) I. (1971) 82:1–80. II. (1972) 89:81–237. III. (1973) 91:239–333.

Mitchell, T. B. 1960. Bees of the Eastern United States. *North Carolina Agricultural Experiment Station Technical Bulletin* 141.

Morris, W. F., M. Price, N. Waser, J. D. Thomson, B. A. Thomson, and D. A. Stratton. 1994. Systematic increase in pollen carryover and its consequences for geitonogamy in plant populations. *Oikos* 7:431–440.

Morse, D. H. 1982. Behavior and ecology of bumble bees. *Social Insects* 3:245–322.

Müller, Christine B. 1994. Parasitoid induced digging behaviour in bumblebee workers. *Animal Behaviour* 48:961–966.

Müller, C. B., J. A. Shykoff, and G. H. Sutcliffe. 1992. Life history patterns and opportunities for queen-worker conflict in bumblebees (Hymenoptera: Apidae). *Oikos* 65:242–248.

Müller, H. 1883. *The Fertilisation of Flowers*. (D.W. Thompson, trans.). Macmillan, London. 669 pp.

Nabhan, G. P. and S. L. Buchmann. 1997. Services provided by pollinators. In *Nature's Services: Societal Dependence on Natural Ecosystems*. G. C. Daily, ed. Island Press, Washington, D.C. pp. 133–150.

Neff, J. L. and B. B. Simpson. 1993. Bees, pollination systems and plant diversity. In *Hymenoptera and Biodiversity*. J. LaSalle and I. D. Gauld, eds. CAB International, Wallingford, U.K. pp. 143–168.

Newsholme, E. A., B. Crabtree, S. J. Higgins, S. D. Thornton, and C. Start. 1972. The activities of fructose diphosphatase in flight muscles from the bumblebee and the role of this enzyme in heat generation. *Biochemical Journal* 128:89–97.

Ono, M., M. Mitsuhata and M. Sasaki. 1994. Use of introduced *Bombus terrestris* worker helpers for rapid development of Japanese native *B. hypocrita* colonies (Hymenoptera, Apidae). *Applied Entomology and Zoology* 29:413–419.

Osborne, J. L., I. H. Williams, and S. A. Corbet. 1991. Bees, pollination and habitat change in the European Community. *Bee World* 72:99–116.

Osborne, J. L., S. J. Clark, R. J. Morris, I. H. Williams, J. R. Riley, A. D. Smith, D. R. Reynolds, and A. S. Edwards. 1999. A landscape-scale study of bumble bee foraging range and constancy, using harmonic radar. *Journal of Applied Ecology* 36:519–533.

O'Toole, C. 1993. Diversity of native bees and agroecosystems. In *Hymenoptera and Biodiversity*. J. LaSalle and I. D. Gauld, eds. CAB International, Wallingford, U.K. pp. 169–196.

O'Toole, C. and A. Raw. 1991. *Bees of the World.* Blandford Publishing, Facts on File, Inc., New York. 192 pp.

Owen, R. E. and L. Packer. 1994. Estimation of the proportion of diploid males in populations of Hymenoptera. *Heredity* 72:219–227.

Owen, R. E., K. W. Richards, and A. Wilkes. 1995. Chromosome numbers and karyotypic variation in bumble bees (Hymenoptera: Apidae; Bombini). *Journal of the Kansas Entomological Society* 68: 290–302.

Peach, M. L., V. J. Tepedino, D. G. Alston, and T. L. Griswold. 1993. Insecticide treatments for rangeland grasshoppers: Potential effects on the reproduction of *Pediocactus sileri* (Englem.) Benson (Cactaceae). In *Proceedings Southwestern Rare and Endangered Plant Conference.* R. Sivinski and K. Lightfoot, eds. New Mexico Forestry and Resources Conservation Division, Miscellaneous Publication Number 2. Santa Fe, New Mexico. pp. 309–333.

Peterson, R. T. 1947. *A Field Guide to the Birds.* Houghton Mifflin Company, Boston. 230 pp.

Plath, O. E. 1927. The Natural grouping of the Bremidae (Bombidae) with special reference to biological characters. *Biological Bulletin* 52:394–410.

Plath, O. E. 1934. *Bumblebees and Their Ways.* Macmillan, New York. 201 pp.

Pleasants, J. M. 1989. Optimal foraging by nectarivores: A test of the marginal-value theorem. *American Naturalist* 134:51–71.

Plowright, R. C. and T. M. Laverty. 1984. The ecology and sociobiology of bumble bees. *Annual Review of Entomology* 29:175–199.

Plowright, R. C. and F. H. Rodd. 1980. The effect of aerial spraying on hymenopterous pollinators in New Brunswick. *Canadian Entomologist* 112:259–269.

Possingham, H. P. 1989. The distribution and abundance of resources encountered by a forager. *American Naturalist* 133:42–60.

Prys-Jones, O. E. and S. A. Corbet. 1991. *Bumblebees.* Naturalists' Handbooks 6. Richmond Publishing Co. Ltd., Slough, U.K. 92 pp.

Pyke, G. H. 1978a. Optimal foraging in bumblebees and coevolution with their plants. *Oecologia* 36:281–293.

Pyke, G. H. 1978b. Optimal foraging-movement patterns of bumblebees between inflorescences. *Theoretical Population Biology* 13:72–98.

Pyke, G. H. 1982. Local geographic distributions of bumblebees near Crested Butte, Colorado: competition and community structure. *Ecology* 63:555–573.

Pyke, G. H. and R. V. Cartar. 1992. The flight directionality of bumblebees: Do they remember where they came from? *Oikos* 65:321–327.

Real, L. A. 1981. Uncertainty and pollinator-plant interactions-the foraging behavior of bees and wasps on artificial flowers. *Ecology* 62:20–26.

Richards, K. W. 1978. Nest site selection by bumblebees (Hymenoptera: Apidae) in Southern Alberta. *Canadian Entomologist* 110:301–318.

Richards, K. W. 1993. Non-*Apis* bees as crop pollinators. *Revue Suisse Zoologie* 100:807–822.

Richards, O. W. 1968. The subgeneric division of the Genus *Bombus* Latreille (Hymenoptera: Apidae). *Bulletin of the British Museum* (Natural History) 22(5):211–276.

Rodd, F. H., R. C. Plowright, and R. E. Owen. 1980. Mortality-rates of adult bumble bee workers (Hymenoptera, Apidae). *Canadian Journal of Zoology* 58:1718–1721.

Röseler, P. F. 1985. A technique for year-round rearing of *Bombus terrestris* (Apidae, Bombini) colonies in captivity. *Apidologie* 16:165–169.

Sampson, A. W. 1952. *Range Management: Principles and Practices.* Wiley, New York.

Schmid-Hempel, P. 1998. *Parasites in Social Insects.* Princeton University Press, Princeton, New Jersey. 409 pp.

Schmid-Hempel, P. and S. Durrer. 1991. Parasites, floral resources and reproduction in natural populations of bumblebees. *Oikos* 62:342–350.

Schmid-Hempel, P., C. Müller, R. Schmid-Hempel, and J. A. Shykoff. 1990. Frequency and ecological correlates of parasitism by conopid flies (Conopidae, Diptera) in populations of bumblebees. *Insectes Sociaux* 37:14–30.

Seton, Ernest Thompson. 1991. *Wild Animals I Have Known.* McClelland and Stewart, Toronto. Reprinted from original version published by Charles Scribner's Sons, 1898. New York. 357 pp.

Shykoff, J. A. and C. B. Müller. 1995. Reproductive decisions in bumble-bee colonies: The influence of worker mortality in *Bombus terrestris* (Hymenoptera, Apidae). *Functional Ecology* 9:106–112.

Shykoff, Jacqui A. and P. Schmid-Hempel. 1991. Parasites delay worker reproduction in bumblebees: Consequences for eusociality. *Behavioral Ecology* 2:242–248.

Sipes, S. D. and V. J. Tepedino 1995. Reproductive biology of the rare orchid, *Spiranthes diluvialis:* Breeding system, pollination, and implications for conservation. *Conservation Biology* 9:929–938.

Sladen, F.W.L. 1912. *The Humble-bee, Its Life History and How to Domesticate It.* Macmillan, New York (reprinted in 1989 by Logaston Press, Woonton, U.K.).

Sugden, E. A. 1985. Pollinators of *Astragalus monoensis* Barneby (Fabaceae): New host records; potential impact of sheep grazing. *Great Basin Naturalist* 45(2):299–312.

Tepedino, V. J. 1979. The importance of bees and other insect pollinators in maintaining floral species composition. *Great Basin Naturalist Memoirs Number 3*: The Endangered Species: A symposium; 7–8 Dec. 1978. Brigham Young University, Provo, Utah. pp. 39–150.

Thomson, J. D. 1981. Field measures of flower constancy in bumblebees. *American Midland Naturalist* 105:377–380.

Thomson, J. D. 1986. Pollen transport and deposition by bumble bees in *Erythronium:* Influences of floral nectar and bee grooming. *Journal of Ecology*

74:329–341.

Thomson, J. D. 1996. Trapline foraging by bumblebees: I. Persistence of flight-path geometry. *Behavioral Ecology* 7:158–164.

Thomson, J. D., W. P. Maddison, and R. C. Plowright. 1982. Behavior of bumble bee pollinators of *Aralia hispida* Vent. (Araliaceae). *Oecologia* 54:326–336.

Thomson, J. D., S. Peterson, and L. Harder. 1987. Response of traplining bumble bees to competition experiments: Shifts in feeding location and efficiency. *Oecologia* 71:295–300.

Thomson, J. D., M. Slatkin, and B. A. Thomson. 1997. Trapline foraging by bumble bees: II. Definition and detection from sequence data. *Behavioral Ecology* 8:199–210.

Thorp, R. W., D. S. Horning, and L. L Dunning. 1983. Bumble bees and cuckoo bumble bees of California (Hymenoptera: Apidae). *Bulletin of the California Insect Survey*, Volume 23.

van Heemert, C., A. de Ruijter, and J. van den Eijnde. 1990. Year-round production of bumble bee colonies for crop pollination. *Bee World* 71:54–56.

Vetter, R. S. and P. K. Vissher. 1998. Bites and stings of medically important venomous arthropods. *International Journal of Dermatology* 37:481–496. *http://spiders.ucr.edu/dermatol.html*; September 2000.

Waddington, K. D. 1980. Flight patterns of foraging bees relative to density of artificial flowers and distribution of nectar. *Oecologia* 44:199–204.

Waddington, K. D. and B. Heinrich. 1979. The foraging movements of bumble-bees on vertical "inflorescences": An experimental analysis. *Journal of Comparative Physiology* 134:113–117.

Waser, N. M. 1986. Flower constancy: Definition, cause and measurement. *American Naturalist* 127:593–603.

Washitani, I. 1996. Predicted genetic consequences of strong fertility selection due to pollinator loss in an isolated population of *Primula sieboldii*. *Conservation Biology* 10:59–64.

Williams, C. S. 1995. Conserving Europe's bees: Why all the buzz. *Trends in Ecology and Evolution* 10:309–310.

Williams, I. H., S. A. Corbet, and J. L. Osborne. 1991. Beekeeping, wild bees and pollination in the European community. *Bee World* 72:170–180.

Williams, N. M. and J. D. Thomson. 1998. Trapline foraging by bumble bees: III. Temporal patterning of visits. *Behavioral Ecology* 9:612–621.

Williams, P. H. 1982. The distribution and decline of British bumble bees (*Bombus* Latr.). *Journal of Apicultural Research* 21(4):236–245.

Williams, P. H. 1985. A preliminary cladistic investigation of relationships among the bumblebees (Hymenoptera, Apidae). *Systematic Entomology* 10:239–255.

Williams, P. H. 1986. Environmental change and the distributions of British bumble bees (*Bombus* Latr.). *Bee World* 67:50–61.

Williams, P. H. 1998. An annotated checklist of bumble bees with an analysis of patterns of description (Hymenoptera: Apidae, Bombini). *Bulletin of Natural History Museum, London (Ent.)* 67:79–152.

Wilson, E. O. 1971. *The Insect Societies.* Belknap Press of Harvard University, Cambridge, Massachusetts. 548 pp.

Index ──────────────────────

Page numbers in italics indicate illustrations.